ASHLEY DAVIS BUSH LICSW

THE ART *&* POWER
OF ACCEPTANCE

Your Guide to Inner Peace

To Maria,

A beacon of light

STERLING ETHOS
New York

An Imprint of Sterling Publishing Co., Inc.
1166 Avenue of the Americas
New York, NY 10036

Text © 2019 Ashley Davis Bush

ISBN 978-1-4549-3792-0

Distributed in Canada by Sterling Publishing Co., Inc.
c/o Canadian Manda Group, 664 Annette Street
Toronto, Ontario M6S 2C8, Canada

For information about custom editions, special
sales, and premium and corporate purchases, please
contact Sterling Special Sales at 800-805-5489
or specialsales@sterlingpublishing.com.

Manufactured in China

2 4 6 8 10 9 7 5 3 1

sterlingpublishing.com

Design by Miranda Harvey

Cover: front, Maria-Galybina/istock; back, Oksancia/istock
Picture Credits – see page 224

Disclaimer
While the road toward accepting the unacceptable
(whether people, the past, or circumstances) eventually
leads to inner peace, it can trigger, for some, powerful
feelings of deep-rooted trauma along the way. This
book is meant to be a guide, but if you're having an
unusually difficult time coping or if you're feeling stuck,
overwhelmed, or even paralyzed, please reach out for
professional assistance. Therapeutic companionship
can make all the difference in helping you along the
road of healing.

About the author
Ashley Davis Bush, LICSW is a psychotherapist with
30 years of experience in the mental health field. She
is a freelance writer and the author of eight self-help
books, including *The Little Book of Inner Peace*.
She is also a grief counsellor and an expert in stress
management, self-care, and self-compassion skills.
She lives in New Hampshire with her husband, also
a psychotherapist. They have five grown children.

CONTENTS

Prologue 6

1

The Process—Resistance to Alignment to Possibility 23

2

The Key—Self-compassion 49

3

Accepting Yourself 81

4

Accepting Others 109

5

Accepting Your Circumstances 133

6

Accepting the Past 157

7

Living with Possibility 183

Epilogue 210

References and Further Reading 220

Index 222

Acknowledgements and Picture Credits 224

Acceptance takes grace and courage, a choice that is made moment by moment. It isn't always the obvious path but is a solution with empowerment potential beyond your wildest dreams.

PROLOGUE

"If I could define enlightenment briefly, I would say it is 'the quiet acceptance of what is'."

WAYNE DYER

One day I was having lunch with a dear friend. Over tortellini drenched in a gorgonzola cream sauce, I learned that her new business coach had challenged her to sum up her work in a single word.

"You've heard of an elevator pitch?" she asked. I had. It's a concise but compelling summary that lasts no longer than a short elevator ride. "Well", she added, "this is more like an elevator-closing-in-your-face pitch."

Curious. She went on to explain that the purpose of the exercise wasn't for marketing purposes but for personal clarity. By distilling your business into one word, you highlight the essence and purpose of your work.

My friend, a singing teacher and speaking coach, came down to the word "voice". A doctor in her mastermind group had drilled down to the word "heal"; a financial advisor "wealth"; a jeweler "adorn"; a restaurateur "nourish".

"What word do you think would sum up your work?" she continued. "Something like 'change'?"

Hmmmmm, change. There is no doubt that people call me when they are in crisis, desperate for change. A specific trigger arises—a feeling gets too intense, a relationship gets too challenging, a circumstance becomes intolerable—and they reach out for help.

As I reflected on 30 years of treating grief, loneliness, anxiety, distressed relationships, depression, and stress, I realized that while change had often happened, it wasn't at the center of my work. There was something more basic, a precursor to change. At the heart of my work was something subtler yet ultimately more liberating.

"I would have to say that my word", I ventured as I sipped my coffee, "is not change." I reflected a moment longer. "My word is 'acceptance'."

My friend shook her head, miffed. "Acceptance? But don't your clients come to you for change?"

"The irony", I replied, "is that when someone intentionally chooses acceptance, everything begins to change."

That night, I mused on the essence of "acceptance"—being with what is as it is. I realized that not only is it the perfect word to describe the core of my work with clients, but it is also probably the most powerful, most unexpected life skill for peace and well-being. Active acceptance surprisingly leads to emotional liberation.

THE QUEST FOR RELIEF

But when you are suffering in your life, you probably don't want to hear about acceptance. Even now you might be thinking, *Wait, I'm miserable and suffering and I'm desperate to feel better. If I accept my reality as it is, nothing will change. I'll fall even deeper into a pit of despair.* Admittedly, at first glance, acceptance doesn't really sound all that compelling. It doesn't have the pure ring of "joy" and "happiness". It doesn't sound as hopeful as "optimism" or "resilience". It's not as convincing as "success" or "transformation". And yet it is the surprising path to all of these.

Acceptance gets a bad rap, actually, since it is so often confused with resignation, defeat or, worse, completely giving up. But acceptance doesn't mean tolerating abuse, condoning injustice, or staying mired in pathology. Nor does acceptance mean that you approve of what's going on or even remotely like it. Acceptance is a calming orientation toward your reality, a shift in perspective in which struggle dissolves, opposition relaxes, and clarity dawns.

Consider this book your invitation to think differently about acceptance and to open yourself to a new way of relating to your life. I believe that you'll discover for yourself that acceptance isn't about giving up or being stuck. Instead, it is about active alignment with your feelings and your situation, and then an opening to something more. **Acceptance is the paradigm shift that leads to every experience of lasting inner peace.**

We've all been in a place of struggling against the tide—resisting our difficult circumstances, wishing things were otherwise, regretting things said and unsaid, judging our shortcomings. After all the years of struggle and forceful attempts to change ourselves, other people, our circumstances, and even our past, acceptance turns out to be the path of sanity and wisdom. It lifts us up to a place of wider perspective and vision where we can open-heartedly acknowledge the vista before us, just as it is. **And, then, possibility arises.**

RELEASING THE ROPE

Imagine yourself in a beautiful field holding onto a rope; you're in a tug-of-war. On the other end of the rope is a veiled figure and it's pulling hard. You tug on your end even harder. Your opponent is actually life itself, pulling you toward circumstances that you don't like or want: a traffic jam, weight gain, a long line to wait in, an annoying boss, an alcoholic mother, a cancer diagnosis, an unexpected death. *No! I can't stand it!* You didn't ask for this to happen, this mildly annoying to totally tragic circumstance, this irritating person—all making your life wretched. You yank harder at the rope.

If I pull hard enough, you think, I can get this damn rope to stay put. I can control it.

The trouble is that life, your alleged adversary, always pulls harder than you. The rope never stays still. Things keep happening that you don't want, didn't ask for and can't stop. It can feel at times ridiculously frustrating, exhausting, excruciating and downright heartbreaking. In Buddhism, there is a name for this—the First Noble Truth, which acknowledges that life is hard.

But what if there were a way to halt the battle? What if you could simply stop resisting the pull and relax? What if something simple could assist you with letting it be? Imagine the sweet relief you would feel if you could stop the rope burn—simply open your fingers and watch the rope follow its natural trajectory. Yes, just let it go. When you accept life on its terms—when you stop pulling on your end of the rope—then you can just sit down in that field...be at peace...and, well, smell the flowers.

This book is about how to let go of the rope. It's about the inner art and life-changing power of acceptance, your direct path to a more peaceful, satisfying life experience. The art of acceptance is inherent in the unique and creative ways in which you individualize your journey. The power of acceptance is evident as you discover a kinder relationship both with yourself and with life.

> **"Out beyond ideas of wrongdoing and rightdoing, there is a field. I'll meet you there."**
>
> RUMI

HOW ACCEPTANCE MAKES ALL THE DIFFERENCE

Lydia and Samantha are two bereaved parents, both in their late 40s, with whom I worked years ago. They didn't know each other, yet they had strikingly similar lives.

Lydia had suffered the tragic loss of her 20-year-old daughter 3 years previously. Her daughter had struggled for years with a heroin addiction. It seemed that she was doing better after a successful stint in rehab. Then, unexpectedly, one summer night, her daughter overdosed.

Samantha had suffered the tragic loss of her 18-year-old son in an automobile accident, also 3 years previously. He had just graduated from high school, and life had been full of promise. He was hit by a drunk driver and killed instantly.

But the similarities between them extended even beyond their tragic losses. Both Lydia and Samantha had been sexually abused as children— one by an uncle and the other by a neighbor. Both Lydia and Samantha were also slightly overweight and suffered from type 2 diabetes. And finally, both Lydia and Samantha lived near their overbearing, highly strung mothers. Here their similarities ended.

In our work together, Lydia remained locked in her anger. She blamed herself for her daughter's addiction and continued reliving every detail before the overdose, berating herself for not being able to stop the tragic outcome. Unable to forgive herself, she became depressed as she turned her rage inward. Simultaneously, she stewed in resentment about her horrendous childhood, as she was unable to make sense of the sexual abuse that she had endured.

I sat with Lydia in her grief, but she was unable to fully acknowledge the pain beneath her rage. I taught her mindfulness, self-compassion, and peace practices, but they didn't stick. She continued to spiral downward, railing against the fact that her daughter had died. Bitter and tense, Lydia often binged on sugar despite her medical complications. She frequently got into huge arguments with her mother. The harder life pulled, the harder Lydia yanked on her end of the rope. When Lydia stopped coming to sessions, I felt disappointed that I hadn't been able to help her.

Samantha, on the other hand, was able to acknowledge the depth and breadth of her sorrow. Open to the natural flow of grief, she was able to take the mindfulness and self-compassion practices that I suggested and integrate them into her life. She treated herself gently and learned to tolerate the searing pain she felt as a result of her loss.

Life was pulling, but Samantha didn't resist; she released the rope. She didn't get stuck in her grief—rather, she let it flow and wash over her. Eventually, she turned toward the possibilities that arose from her experience. She started advocating for stricter drink-driving laws and became active in a bereaved parents' organization called The Compassionate Friends (see page 160).

When Samantha started to feel hijacked by guilt or self-loathing (both natural human emotions), she wrapped her feelings in the gentle embrace of self-compassion, which allowed the hostile emotions to dissipate. She integrated her past and present, seeing that all experiences were part of her journey to the present moment. Feeling more warmth toward herself, she changed her diet and began to exercise regularly. Her renewed relationship with herself offered her the clarity to set up boundaries with her mother and not take her mother's behavior so personally.

Samantha stopped resisting her circumstances by accepting her feelings and opening up to her reality. As a result, she was freed to create her own *better* reality. Lydia, on the other hand, had kept her heart closed and defensive, resistant to her pain and the truth of loss. While these women had lived with similar life circumstances, they ultimately had radically different experiences.

“Samantha integrated her past and present, seeing that all experiences were part of her journey to the present moment.”

THERE IS A KEY

Acceptance, as a time-honored path of emotional and spiritual healing, is not a new idea. It is widely recognized in both modern psychology and sacred texts as a liberating goal. But, here's the thing—getting there can be really hard. Clearly, it isn't as simple as snapping your fingers or saying to yourself, *Get over it*. Acceptance can feel challenging, painful, and downright impossible. How do you accept the unacceptable?

What I've noticed in my many years as a psychotherapist is that *everything* starts with the self. Whether you're accepting another person, a circumstance or something from the past, acceptance begins with you, your *feelings* about that situation and, most importantly, how you treat yourself. When you can be compassionate with yourself, you more easily accept reality. **Self-compassion is the key that unlocks the door to acceptance.**

That is the essence of this book: self-compassion—acceptance—peace. Highlighting the skill of self-compassion, employing its scientifically demonstrated benefits, harnessing the capacity of the higher self—all of this enables us to move from resistance to alignment to possibility. Although your journey will be unique, this book offers you a map to improve your relationship with yourself and your relationship with life.

"Everything *starts with the self.*"

HOW THIS BOOK WORKS

Each of us can choose to surrender the rope of life, not denying the facts but learning new ways to work with them. In the pages that follow, you will see how acceptance can become your new mindset.

In Chapter 1, we look at **the map of the journey**, learning about acceptance as a process leading from resistance to alignment to possibility. Chapter 2 spotlights the skill of **self-compassion** as the essential guide along the road. When you learn to accept your feelings and be kind to yourself in the process, you disarm resistance and are then able to move forward to possibility.

Chapters 3 to 6 explore specific life applications of acceptance: **accepting yourself, accepting others, accepting your circumstances, and accepting the past**. While it might be a breeze to accept fun, happy things such as promotions, engagements, financial windfalls, and exotic vacations, we know that life is full of many difficult circumstances. Here we talk about accepting what feels *unacceptable*: abuse, annoying ex-spouses, sickness, self-loathing, addiction, infidelity, loss, even death. Self-compassion is the go-to practice, over and over again, that helps you keep the acceptance process moving.

While aligning with your reality is part of the journey, it's not the whole journey. Eventually, you come to the pivotal question of *now what?* Chapter 7 looks in more detail at that question, at **the power**

of possibility, at what you can change and how. Our culture tends to approve of resistance and aggression as optimal approaches to change. But just as you catch more flies with honey than vinegar, the change that blossoms out of acceptance is sweeter and infinitely more delicious. Here you will discover the dawning of hope.

Each chapter is threaded with personal stories and clinical vignettes (names and details have been changed for privacy). These stories illustrate the range of intensity with which we can experience acceptance in our lives. For some, alignment with the present moment, just as it is, will be without fanfare, a shrug of the shoulders and a nod (*Okay, it is what it is*). For others, alignment will feel like a friendship, a sort of metaphorical handshake (*Oh, hello, come in*). And for others still, the experience of alignment will be a big bear hug, a warm embrace, a sense of enthusiastic welcome (*I love this! Bring it on!*). Chapters 3 to 7 each end with a reflection on a more intense response, showing how you can **"kick it up a notch"**, taking acceptance to a transcendent level.

At the conclusion of each chapter, I share essential **"power tools"** to help you integrate the material more deeply into your own life. I offer a primary tool as well as the option to expand your practice with two bonus tools.

With acceptance, even though
nothing changes, *everything* changes.

THE TIME IS NOW

Acceptance feels like a big long exhale...ahhhhhhhh. With acceptance, you choose to go with the flow of the current instead of swimming against it. Active acceptance, grounded in self-compassion, is about turning toward yourself with an embrace and turning toward life with a smile. It's about living life with less stress, less tension and more flow, more ease.

If you've been striving for change, pushing for something different, but you keep failing time after time...if you've been beating yourself up because you can't seem to implement any of the things you know will help you feel better...if you're tired of pretending that something *isn't* when it clearly *is* (or vice versa), then it's time for a new direction.

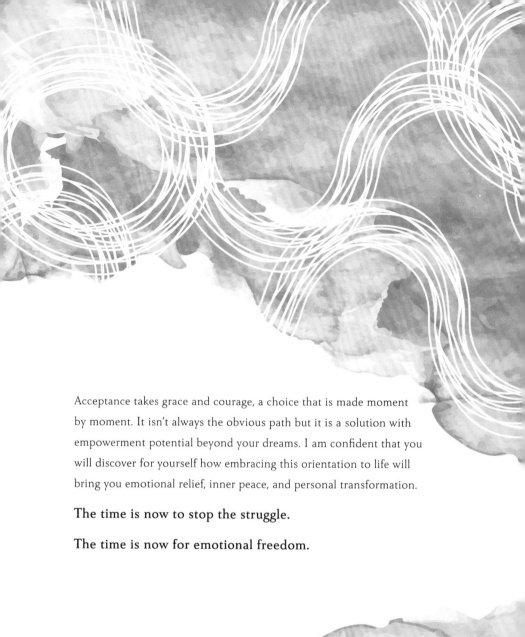

Acceptance takes grace and courage, a choice that is made moment by moment. It isn't always the obvious path but it is a solution with empowerment potential beyond your dreams. I am confident that you will discover for yourself how embracing this orientation to life will bring you emotional relief, inner peace, and personal transformation.

The time is now to stop the struggle.

The time is now for emotional freedom.

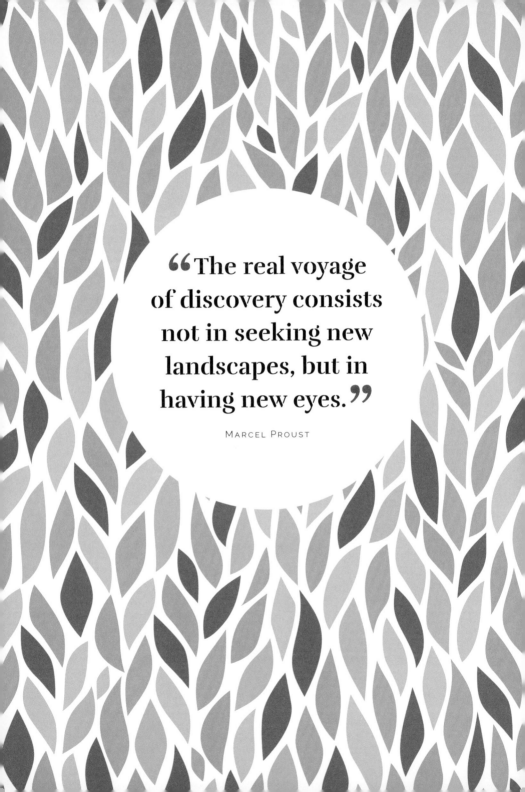

"The real voyage of discovery consists not in seeking new landscapes, but in having new eyes."

MARCEL PROUST

1

THE PROCESS—RESISTANCE TO ALIGNMENT TO POSSIBILITY

We were sitting on the tarmac. We had just landed in Tulsa, Oklahoma, rerouted because of thunderstorms in Dallas.

The captain made an announcement: "Ah, folks, it looks like we're going to be here for a while due to passing weather conditions. Thank you for your patience and I'll be back shortly with an update."

People around me started coming unglued. The captain came back on: "Just a reminder that we will not be exiting the airplane. Please stay in your seats, although you are welcome to stand and stretch."

I was in the first row of the plane so, as I stood to stretch my legs, I got the flight attendant's view of minor passenger mayhem. One by one, people began filing up to the front of the plane and projecting their frustration onto the flight attendants. Passengers proclaimed, "I've got a connection!", "I want off the plane!", "How long will we be here?".

The flight attendant near me kept her cool and said, "We will get you to Dallas safely as soon as we can. We can't control the weather."

One man, particularly frustrated, yelled at this poor woman. "I have a meeting this afternoon. I have got to get to Dallas now!"

"Sir", she repeated, with impressive restraint. "We all want to get to Dallas as quickly as possible, but we cannot control the weather."

The man finally went back to his seat, red-faced. I looked around and could see a distinct difference between those who were accepting our fate and those who were not. The passengers who were stuck in resistance looked anxious, angry, frustrated, impatient and exasperated. The ones who were aligning with the situation looked calm, relaxed, and peaceful. They had moved on by reading and texting.

Why is it that, in a situation that is beyond everyone's control, some people are hijacked (so to speak) by their resistance and others are able to flow? Of course, we all know that choosing acceptance is often easier said than done. If you had been on the plane, how do you think you would have reacted?

THE CONUNDRUM OF ACCEPTANCE

The Latin root word of "accept" means "to take toward yourself".
This sense of bringing in/receiving is at the heart of what I mean by
acceptance—anything from barely tolerating to enthusiastically embracing.
Frequently, we see our present circumstance as an obstacle, a horror, an
inconvenience, something to be rejected. The last thing we want to do is
receive it. So we either complain incessantly or move heaven and earth to
change it. In a culture that encourages constant improvement and striving,
acceptance is often mistakenly seen as a last resort, like a consolation prize.
*You mean just accept that I'm old or that I'm in debt? Accept that my boss is
an idiot? Simply accept that my son died?*

As we reflect on what acceptance is, our understanding can be enhanced
by analysing what it is *not*. Acceptance is not weak resignation or apathy.
Acceptance does not mean you like the current state of affairs. And
acceptance does not condone bad behavior or assume change is impossible.

Acceptance is a bit like forgiveness in that way. Forgiving someone for unspeakable behavior does not mean that what they did was okay. Forgiveness doesn't mean that you honor their choices. It means you accept that what's done is done; you let go and move on. That's how people are able to forgive murderers and molesters—they choose to be free of smoldering anger and resentment, for their own sake. Acceptance is a similar choice—for freedom's sake.

66 *Acceptance is your choice, an active choice.* **99**

THE JOURNEY

In the popular 12-Step model of recovery from addiction—created by Alcoholics Anonymous and now used in many 12-step programs of recovery from addiction and compulsive behavior—acceptance is the **beginning** point. (Step one: "We admitted we were powerless over alcohol—that our lives had become unmanageable.")

In the popular Elisabeth Kübler-Ross model of the five stages of grief in terminal illness (denial, anger, bargaining, depression, acceptance), described in her 1969 book *On Death and Dying*, acceptance is the **ending** point.

In this book, we will explore acceptance from the perspective of a three-stage journey that begins with **resistance**, then shifts into **alignment**, and ends with **possibility**.

SELF-
COMPASSION;
SHIFT;
ACT

Resistance

ENTRY POINT

SELF

OTHERS;
CIRCUMSTANCES;
PAST

28

CHANGE
SITUATION

Possibility

CHANGE
ORIENTATION
TO SITUATION

Alignment

In a nutshell, think of
resistance as "No",
alignment as "Yes" and
possibility as "Next?"

Let's say that you have a terrible head cold, a really nasty one. You might start by **resisting** it with an unwillingness to acknowledge its reality: *No! I can't get sick; I don't have time to be sick; I hate being sick; I wish I wasn't sick.* At some point, you move to **alignment**—you begin to acknowledge that your body is sick and that you are suffering: *okay, I'm sick. I'm really sick. This is my reality. I feel miserable.* In the final phase, as you go with the flow, **possibilities** arise and you begin to notice your options: *I could take medication; I could sleep; I could take a few days off; I could warm up a can of chicken soup. I could watch that TV show I've been meaning to watch.* Acceptance takes us from suffering to peace to possibility. Now let's unpack each part of the process in more detail...

"Acceptance takes us from suffering to peace to possibility."

RESISTANCE

I once attended a talk given by the clinical psychiatrist and author Dan Siegel, who spoke eloquently about parenting, neurobiology, meditation, and resilience. He asked us to shut our eyes and just notice our experience as he spoke. We closed our eyes and he said forcefully, "No". Then he repeated it loudly and insistently: "No". He said it seven times.

After a moment, he said more gently, "Yes". Then softly, "Yes", and calmly, "Yes". He said this seven times.

"Now open your eyes", he said. "What was your experience? Let's start with 'No'. What words come to mind?" People in the audience began to call out their collective experience: "I felt closed." "Tense." "I felt myself flinching." "I felt trapped, scolded." "My heart rate escalated."

"And the 'Yes' experience?" he prompted. People around me said, "I felt free." "Expansive." "More open." "Calm." "Lighter." "I felt comforted."

He went on to describe how the "No" state of mind, based on reactivity and resistance, actually stimulates our fear responses of fight, flight, or freeze. Whereas when we operate from the "Yes" state of mind, based in receptivity (aka acceptance), we activate the caring, social-engagement system in the brain. And from there, we experience clarity and calm.

Resistance (the "No" brain) takes an enormous amount of energy and concentration. "No" is both a resistant thought and a powerful nervous system activator. "No" stimulates our sympathetic nervous system (which is responsible for the fight-or-flight response), bathing the brain in a cocktail of stress chemicals—cortisol, adrenaline, and norepinephrine. Resistance is swimming upstream, fighting the current of "what is".

Resistance is feverishly gripping that rope of life, clamping down futilely to stop its motion, and all the while getting severe rope burn. This condition of neurological stress is laborious, exhausting, and painful.

Resistance is what the Buddha called the "second arrow". In a famous parable, he describes the first arrow as whatever painful event life throws your way (a cancer diagnosis, the death of a loved one, getting fired from a job). Those are simply part of life. But the pain we suffer from the second arrow, the dart of resistance (our negative reaction to the first arrow), comes from adding insult to injury with the mindset of *No!* or *It can't be!* or *Why me?* or *I want it to be different—I can't stand this!* As you gnash your teeth and wring your hands, you create the tight, constricted agony of resistance. Your response is adding an additional level of suffering; your reaction is the "second arrow".

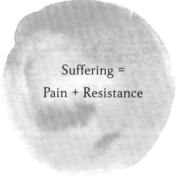

Suffering =
Pain + Resistance

As we all know, fighting reality is *exhausting*. And yet, it's the most common form of suffering. I'm talking about the chronic pain and "dis-ease" (the lack of "ease" or harmony) of wishing things were other than they actually are or were. Resistance is dark and negative; it floods your mind and blinds you to possibility.

The psychiatrist and psychoanalyst Carl Jung said, "What you resist not only persists, but will grow in size". In other words, resistance builds on itself. When you stay with your resistance, you magnify and strengthen its power. But the last thing we want to do is increase the very negative emotions that we're trying to get rid of; who wants *more* resentment, blame, pain, anxiety, or anger? While resistance makes you a victim to the very negativity that you don't want, acceptance releases you. When you let go by turning toward the problem, leaning into it, surrendering to what is, negativity loses its power over you, and peace and healing naturally emerge.

Often, it is the agony of resistance itself that motivates our process of acceptance. Because resistance hurts, in our darkest hours of wrestling with it, we hear a whisper or we feel an impulse that maybe there is a different way to be with this. Maybe there is a way to suffer less. At the edge of this awareness, the light of "alignment" beckons.

"Fighting reality is exhausting."

ALIGNMENT

Aligning with "what is" involves saying "yes"—yes to your current feelings, yes to others as they are and, ultimately, yes to your circumstances. This doesn't mean that you like or approve of what's happening. It simply means that you have come to terms with it because, at the moment, it's what you've got.

The way to feeling at ease with any circumstance is to first accept your feelings about it exactly as they are. You simply allow yourself to be with your experience, even the wish that things were otherwise (the key for doing this is self-compassion—see chapter 2, page 49). As you align with your feelings, compassionately validating your experience, you'll notice that you initiate a sense of flowing *with* rather than *against*...a feeling of relaxation. And when you relax, things shift.

As with the practice of the martial art of aikido, when you flow with aggressive energy that is directed at you, you avoid getting hit and instead redirect the momentum. You effectively neutralize hostility. When you move intentionally with "what is" rather than against it, you create stress-free movement for yourself. This is a process of working with things as they already are instead of wasting energy wishing that they were different.

Imagine the relief of just pausing, breathing, relaxing—*allowing* the "what is" to be as it is, just as it is, in this moment in time. You will find with alignment that even though nothing changes, *everything* changes.

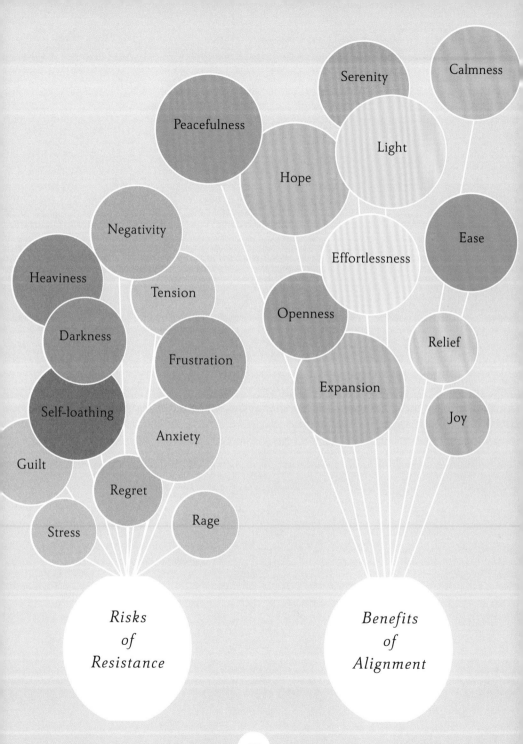

Serenity

Calmness

Peacefulness

Light

Hope

Negativity

Ease

Heaviness

Effortlessness

Tension

Darkness

Openness

Relief

Frustration

Expansion

Self-loathing

Joy

Anxiety

Guilt

Regret

Rage

Stress

*Risks
of
Resistance*

*Benefits
of
Alignment*

Let's take a closer look at how this process of acceptance might unfold. Charlotte, age 45, came to see me after she learned that her husband of 18 years, Jerry, had been having an affair with a colleague at work for the past 6 months. When he was taking a shower, Charlotte saw texts lighting up his phone from the "other woman". She felt as if she had been kicked in the stomach.

She confronted Jerry when he came out of the shower. For several minutes, he denied it and claimed that he had no idea what those texts were. But after Charlotte's persistent ranting and sobbing, he finally admitted what they both already knew was true. Charlotte's idea of her loyal husband and her perfect life collapsed.

Charlotte came to see me with Jerry. Jerry expressed extreme sorrow and was immediately willing to end the affair. I knew this was a positive sign because often I see couples who display very little contrition. Jerry went so far as to get himself transferred to another branch of his company to distance himself from the other woman.

Initially, Charlotte was firm in her stance: "This shouldn't be happening to me and to us." She was squarely—and appropriately—in resistance. She felt betrayed, as her assumptive world had been shattered, leaving her in tremendous pain. Her sympathetic nervous system had been activated to chronic fight mode. Her neurological system was on high alert. She kept ruminating about what had happened and was desperate for details about every encounter. Jerry was willing to provide information but seemed alarmed when it only served to enrage his wife.

Charlotte was in an agonizing place of not accepting him *(I always thought he was honest and dependable)*, not accepting the circumstances *(I wish this had never happened to us)* and not accepting the past *(If only I could go back and change things so that this had never happened)*. She was even having difficulty accepting herself *(I must be a terrible wife)*. She had every form of *un*acceptance possible.

She had no compassion for Jerry, for the other woman, or for herself. Deep down, she was experiencing an unspoken shame, believing that she must have deserved this for being a less-than-perfect wife over the years.

The journey from resistance to alignment took months of work for Charlotte and for Jerry. It also involved many tears and even two months of separation for Charlotte to see that her relentless resistance was interfering with their ability to move forward. As she continued to blame Jerry, blame herself, wish things were otherwise and rehash past actions in a continuous loop, they both remained stuck. I knew that if Charlotte couldn't soften her resistance at some point, then it wouldn't be the affair that destroyed the marriage, but the aftermath. Repair would only follow if she could make the shift to alignment.

> **❝ *If Charlotte couldn't soften her resistance at some point, then it wouldn't be the affair that destroyed the marriage, but the aftermath.* ❞**

BEGINNING TO SHIFT

Self-compassion was key for Charlotte. She began her shift out of resistance by acknowledging, with tenderness and understanding, the magnitude of her pain and loss. She began to drop tenderly into her sorrow without wishing it were otherwise. Her heart opened bit by bit until she finally came to a place of softening, first by alignment with her pain ("this is what I feel") and later by alignment with the actual affair ("this is what I've got").

This process of validating her own experience by simply being with it, rather than trying to talk herself out of it, created a new, self-soothing experience. She allowed in all of her feelings. That which was terrible (her suffering) became an experience of comfort (her own validation). What a relief to honor and be with her experience instead of pushing, resisting, judging, defying.

When we align, feeling by feeling and experience by experience, we reduce the tension and stress in the body and in the mind. Neurologically, alignment is about activating the parasympathetic nervous system (the body's "all is well" system) so that we can rest, relax and recharge. Alignment, even with our own resistant feelings, clears the emotional space that had been occupied by resistance. Within this spaciousness, we are then freed to align peacefully with our circumstances. After that, space is available for something new, for the third stage in the journey—possibility.

THE POSSIBILITY PARADOX

Once we have let go of "No" and moved into "Yes", we've created room for the question "Next?" Only now can we look around, not with fear or anger, but with curiosity, to see what is possible. In other words, at this juncture, with an increased clarity of mind, we have an opportunity to pivot our position—and thus to invite change.

For Charlotte, once she shifted from resistance ("No") to alignment ("Yes"), she was free to move forward ("Next?"). From the position of "Next?" Charlotte and Jerry together worked in earnest to create a "new marriage". Clearly, in the old marriage there were cracks wide enough to let someone else in. Over time, in our sessions together, we unpacked the years of loneliness that had never been named or discussed.

Charlotte was able to see that while she *wasn't* a terrible wife, she had kept much of her inner world separate from Jerry. She had been so busy trying to create a perfect and stress-free home life that she had never shared her concerns, her struggles, her feelings. Nor had she allowed him to participate fully in the raising of their daughter. As a consequence, Jerry had felt isolated, disconnected, and unloved. The result was that both of them lived in separate, lonely spheres.

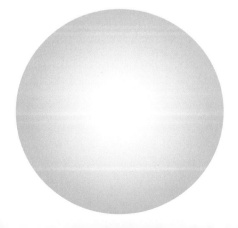

SPACE FOR SOMETHING NEW

After Charlotte and Jerry had acknowledged and accepted their past, the crux of our work moved to creating deeper emotional intimacy and trust. Resting in acceptance, Charlotte could fully absorb Jerry's deep regret and heartfelt apology. From there flowed the terms and conditions and expectations of their new marriage, one in which they would share more openly, talk more freely, and connect more deeply.

By the end of our work together, both Charlotte and Jerry were happier. Charlotte said, "After I first learned about the affair, I remember saying that it was the worst thing that could ever happen to me. Now—well, I wouldn't say it was the best or anything—but I can say it was a wake-up call. Sort of like an alarm bell. And yes, it changed things for us." Smiling, she added, "We get a second chance."

I felt particularly moved by their new-found love. But I also was quick to credit Charlotte for her courage and commitment to her own inner process of acceptance. She had allowed this second chance to happen. Had she remained stuck in resistance, she never could have embraced the possibility of a new marriage. On all fronts, she was able to acknowledge her trauma, align with her feelings and her circumstances, and open her heart to something new. Without that active acceptance process, she and Jerry would have had no chance.

A UNIQUE JOURNEY

From suffering to peace to possibility—the journey of acceptance brings peace to the mind and to the soul. Out of this deep inner peace springs emotional freedom. The process will look different for each of us, depending on background, personality and temperament. In fact, the way each of us navigates the journey is, in itself, a unique exercise in acceptance. **You're going to travel *your* way, and that is the right way for you.**

MOVING FROM "NO" TO "YES"

The trickiest part of the journey to acceptance is stepping from resistance to alignment—actually moving from the "No" to the "Yes". That's the spot where so many of us get stuck. The door to alignment can feel impenetrable. But there is a key that is already in your hands—self-compassion. In the next chapter, that's where we turn our attention.

POWER TOOLS

PRIMARY TOOL: A VISUALIZATION

Sitting quietly with your eyes closed, imagine yourself swimming upstream against a strong current. You struggle wildly against the mighty force, exhausting yourself. Feel the tension in your muscles, the fatigue in your body, the struggle to stay afloat. Feel the water on your face as you gasp for breath. This is **resistance** to the reality of "what is".

Now imagine letting go, releasing the struggle and surrendering yourself to the flow of the current. You turn over on your back, floating, letting yourself be carried by the flow of the water. Feel the sun on your face and the buoyancy of the water, and see the wide blue sky overhead. This is **alignment** with "what is".

Finally, imagine that you are supported by a comfortable raft as you float peacefully downstream...content. You sit up. You look around at the beauty of nature along the shores. What's around that corner? There are a multitude of opportunities to stop and explore if you choose to do so. This is **possibility**.

BONUS TOOL: RELAXING BREATH SEQUENCE

The 4-7-8 breath is an ancient breathing technique that prompts your body to relax, thus recalibrating the central nervous system. When you practice the 4-7-8 restoration breath regularly, over time the effect is a calmer, less reactive disposition.

1 Inhale through your nose to the count of 4.

2 Hold your breath to the count of 7.

3 Exhale through your mouth, as if you were blowing air out through a straw, to the count of 8. You will notice your muscles relax and your heart rate decrease.

4 Immediately repeat the cycle two more times.

Do a three-cycle round in the morning and a three-cycle round in the evening for maximum cumulative effect.

BONUS TOOL: A REFLECTION

Quiet observation relaxes your body and trains your brain in the skill of simple mindful awareness. Choose one of the following reflections.

SKY: Spend a few minutes looking up at the sky or visualizing the sky in your mind's eye. Notice its color. Are there clouds? If so, examine the texture of the clouds. Observe any changes that occur. Try to be like a child full of wonder as you take in the majesty of the sky. Reflect on the sky as a space of no resistance; it allows the clouds, the rain, the dawn and the dusk. Notice your thoughts as if they were clouds. Watch them pass across the sky of your consciousness. Let the sky be your teacher about flow and acceptance.

TREE: Spend a few minutes looking at a tree or visualizing a tree in your mind's eye. Notice the texture of the bark, the color of the leaves, the reflection of light on the tree. Can you hear any sounds or see any movement? Reflect on the fact that the tree does not resist the wind around it, or the rain. The tree doesn't resist when its leaves change color or fall to the ground. Notice how the tree gracefully flows with and receives the forces of nature. Let the tree be your teacher about flow and acceptance.

" *Let the tree be your teacher about flow and acceptance.* **"**

"Wherever you go, go with all your heart."

CONFUCIUS

2

THE KEY—SELF-COMPASSION

Cindy, age 29, sat in front of me blowing her nose. This was our first session together and she was tearfully describing her recent panic attack during a wedding. Meanwhile, her best friend's nuptials were coming up and she was worried that she would have another attack. This time the stakes were higher because she was the maid of honor and would be standing beside the bride. Cindy was terrified that she was going to make a scene and ruin the wedding.

She berated herself, saying, "I'm such a loser, an idiot. Who has panic attacks at weddings?" Blowing her nose, she continued, "This can't keep happening to me. This is a nightmare. I have to make sure it doesn't happen again. What should I do?"

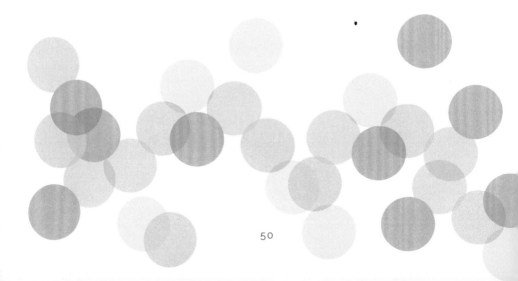

As she talked, I could tell that she was deeply entrenched in resistance—and increasing her anxiety even as she spoke. She was fighting her fear, fighting herself, fighting what might happen. As a result, she was tense and constricted.

I sat in my chair listening to Cindy's distress. As she tried to battle her way out of anxiety, I knew that her path to healing might look different from what she expected. I had treated panic over the years and was aware that she would need to learn to turn toward the panic attacks and accept them, not fight against them. When Cindy changed her relationship to panic attacks they would become less frequent and less distressing.

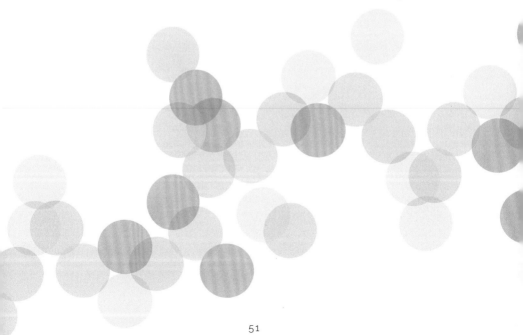

MINDFULNESS AND THE COMPASSIONATE APPROACH

Cindy told me that she didn't want to take medication but was curious about mindfulness, a popular approach she had read about. Mindfulness is a kind of awareness that requires paying attention on purpose. You intentionally notice what is, and you stay present with it. **Mindfulness, by definition, is a form of acceptance.**

The practice of mindfulness is fairly straightforward when it comes to awareness of eating dinner, washing the dishes, or savoring your child's smile. It becomes a bit more challenging, however, when you're trying to be present with a difficult emotion or sensation, such as physical pain, sorrow, fear or, especially, anxiety. Typically, we don't want to pay closer attention to these painful experiences. In fact, our first impulse is the opposite—distraction and escape!

Even with an attitude of nonjudgemental curiosity, it can be hard to stay present with discomfort. So, mindfulness of our pain needs a little assistance, a way of making what feels intolerable a little easier to bear. That boost comes from self-compassion. Think of mindfulness of our inner experience as a kind of sturdy wooden chair. It will support you, but it's a bit uncomfortable. Self-compassion is like a soft cushion that makes the chair more comfortable.

But what exactly is self-compassion? Most people may have a vague idea what it means but they haven't thought too much about it. Some confuse self-compassion with weakness, selfishness, or self-indulgence. **Self-compassion is the gentle and intentional offer of non-judgemental kindness toward yourself. Self-compassion embraces every part of you, even your suffering, just as you are.**

Kristin Neff, a pre-eminent researcher on self-compassion, describes self-compassion as talking to yourself the way you would toward a good friend. Neff's research highlights the many benefits of self-compassion—that it decreases depression, anxiety, and stress, and increases resilience, life satisfaction, and happiness. Her research identifies three core healing components in the practice of self-compassion: mindfulness, common humanity, and kindness.

I have incorporated these components into the core self-compassion practice that I call **ACT** (**A**cknowledge, **C**onnect, **T**alk kindly). Self-compassion can at first feel uncomfortable and awkward, and so I suggest you follow the ACT procedure *as if* you feel compassion toward yourself—even if it's a stretch. Over time, you will start to feel it authentically. Neuroscience research has demonstrated that "neurons that fire together wire together" (as the neuropsychologist Donald Hebb put it). In other words, with practice, self-compassion will become an ingrained habit. Your brain will change gradually so that self-compassion becomes easier, feels natural and paves the way to self-acceptance.

❝Neurons that fire together wire together.❞

DONALD HEBB

A

Acknowledgement is healing and you have the power to offer that to yourself.

USING YOUR INNER SUPERPOWERS

Before I continue with Cindy's story, let's look closely at ACT and the three targeted components of self-compassion.

ACKNOWLEDGEMENT

This refers to saying or thinking something like "Ashley, you're feeling so sad and scared". Acknowledging a feeling is a primary healing agent. Its power comes from relaxing the body and mind.

In the field of neuroscience, this calming phenomenon is known playfully as "name it to tame it". Dan Siegel, author and psychiatrist, explains that when you name your feelings, you activate your "upstairs brain" (the cortex), which literally calms your "downstairs brain" (the subcortex). Why? Because when the cognitive part of you acknowledges your feeling, you secrete soothing neurotransmitters that calm your more primitive, "reptilian" brain. You literally change your body chemistry by acknowledging your feeling.

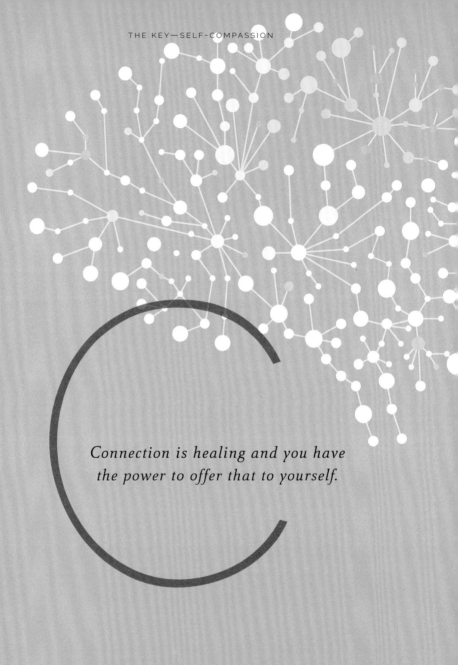

*Connection is healing and you have
the power to offer that to yourself.*

CONNECTION

This refers to saying or thinking something like, "Ashley, you are not alone. Lots of people feel sad and scared, even right at this moment." When you draw your attention to a shared common experience, to the fact that you are not alone, you automatically feel soothed. We are wired for connection and attachment, and we feel better when we remind ourselves that we are part of a larger group.

Shelley E. Taylor, author of *The Tending Instinct*, developed the "tend and befriend" theory of stress response. She observed that people, particularly women, reach out to nurture each other during stressful times. Our brain's social-care circuit primes itself with oxytocin in social situations so that we feel comforted, connected, and supported. By reminding yourself of your connection to others, you effectively activate your own "tend and befriend" neural network, which not only reduces your stress but gives you the feeling of loving connection.

T

Talking kindly to yourself is healing and you have the power to offer that to yourself.

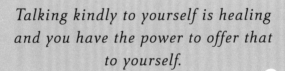

TALKING KINDLY TO YOURSELF

This refers to saying or thinking something like, "Ashley, you're going to be okay. You will get through this." Research demonstrates that it is more powerful and soothing to talk to yourself in the second person than in the first person. Instead of calling yourself "I", using "you" (or your own name) activates the care circuit of the brain and thus generates a greater feeling of self-support. Talking kindly to yourself accesses your "higher self", the part of you that is able to soothe and comfort.

Research in the area of Internal Family Systems (based on the theory that the mind consists of separate subpersonalities), as well as Acceptance and Commitment Therapy, confirms that when you access your "observing self" you're able to experience relief from being caught up in or identified with your own thoughts.

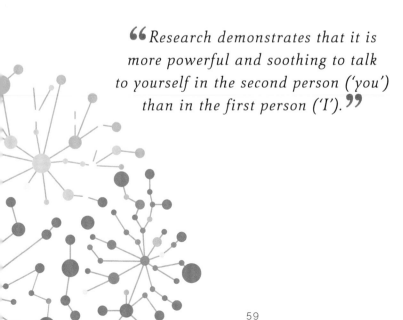

66 *Research demonstrates that it is more powerful and soothing to talk to yourself in the second person ('you') than in the first person ('I').* **99**

ACT IN ACTION

When I first mentioned to Cindy that self-compassion could be an antidote to her fear of having a panic attack, she thought it sounded like a terrible idea. "But if I'm kind to myself", she retorted, "I'll just fall into the pit even more. I need to stop being a stupid wimpy baby."

Ahhhhh, yes. Cindy's habit was to use harsh words to motivate herself, but unfortunately the opposite happened. Kristin Neff's self-compassion research (see page 53) shows that, when we are rough with ourselves, our nervous system actually feels under attack. And when we feel under attack, we naturally move into the stress response of fight, flight, or freeze. We automatically react against the bully within us. However, when we feel supported and encouraged we relax and are able to think clearly. When we experience compassion toward ourselves—even self-compassion—we feel soothed and reassured.

I explained to Cindy how self-compassion could help her, and she warmed to the idea. "What do I have to lose?" she asked. Here's how Cindy used the ACT practice before the wedding, when she was feeling stressed.

Acknowledge your struggle. Cindy said to herself, "This anticipation is so hard for you. You hate having panic attacks and you're so afraid of ruining your best friend's day. This is really, really stressful."

Connect with our shared common humanity. She told herself, "Cindy, you're not the first person in the world to have a panic attack or be afraid of having another. Tons of people suffer this and have for centuries. You are not alone."

Talk kindly to yourself. She said to herself, "Sweetie, you're going to be okay no matter what. You will be surrounded by people you love. You're going to get through this. May you know peace."

So what happened to Cindy? Did she have a panic attack during the wedding? Yes—but not during the ceremony. It happened afterward, during the dinner. But instead of thinking, *This shouldn't be happening*, she naturally launched right into the ACT practice, **acknowledging** that "Cindy, you're suffering. This is really hard." She soothed herself

by **connecting** with others, reminding herself that "Lots of people have panic attacks. You're not alone." And she sidestepped the thought *You're a loser* and instead used **talking kindly** to herself, saying, "You'll be just fine. You're a strong woman and you'll get through this."

For Cindy, the evening was a triumph because she hadn't fallen apart, even *with* a brief panic attack. She had managed just fine and the wave of anxiety had lasted only minutes rather than half the night. Her relationship with herself and her anxiety was changing; she was becoming her own best friend.

As Cindy walked in my door the week after the wedding, she blurted out, with a smile on her face, "I never imagined not panicking about the panic."

"Before our work together," she continued, "I probably would have left during the dinner. I would have been a wreck. Instead, I was fine and I stayed for the whole event."

"And guess what?" she added, grinning. "I caught the wedding bouquet!"

RESISTING RESISTANCE

Resistance is a battle, an opposition that depletes your energy and robs you of your peace of mind. When Cindy first came to see me, she was lodged squarely in resistance. She hated the panic attacks and was desperate to stop them. She couldn't imagine aligning with anxiety and was firmly entrenched in "No, this has to stop happening".

When we are in resistance (wishing something were other than it is), we experience a hardness, a closed heart, a fevered thrashing against our own reality. To have compassion for this experience, for the essence of the struggle, is to shift toward alignment. We accept resistance without trying to change it or make it go away. Ah, validation. The heart relaxes a bit and, paradoxically, the resistance begins to dissipate.

You might think of resistance as a small, scared child who is hiding in the closet, cowering. When you acknowledge them gently and honor their fear, when you offer compassion, they feel seen and accepted. When you hold them in your arms so they know they're safe, they can rest. As you create a sense of unity with that frightened part of yourself, that inner child, there is no more struggle. You can sigh, *Yes, someone gets it.* Space opens within you.

We are all unique in our attempts to protect ourselves and relieve ourselves of suffering. We each have our own individual histories, our own distinctive brains and our own ways of coping with life. Self-compassion, like acceptance, is a creative process, an art that will look and feel a little different for everyone.

66 Self-compassion, like acceptance, is a creative process, an art that will look and feel a little different for everyone. 99

YOU'VE GOT A FRIEND IN YOU

Compassion comes from our innate capacity to love others. Self-compassion is the turning of that loving attention inward. From it comes the feeling that someone understands your pain and knows how to soothe it: you.

Because what you practice consistently gets stronger over time, self-compassion will become your new default response. As your sense of struggle lessens, as resistance falls away, as you feel supported by yourself, you are free to shift into the spaciousness of alignment with the world around you.

Let's say that you're caught in a traffic jam and you're late for work. You know that your boss is going to give you a hard time for being late... again. Your experience is resistance—*No, this can't be. I can't be late. I'm going to get in so much trouble.* You might hit the steering wheel in frustration. The anger of your resistance spikes in your body and you feel flushed and agitated. This makes sense; it's your natural response to feeling trapped.

At this juncture, you use **ACT,** your secret self-compassion key.
You **acknowledge** your struggle ("You're in a dreadful situation and
it's really hard"), you **connect** to others in the same situation ("You're
not the only one in this traffic jam; we're all inconvenienced; traffic jams
are part of life") and you **talk kindly** to yourself, drenching yourself in
kindness ("You'll be okay. Everything is just fine. This too shall pass.").
As you offer compassion to yourself, you take the charge out of your
negativity. Your muscles relax and your heart rate comes down. You feel
less alone. Your resistance dissolves, freeing you to move into alignment
with the reality of your situation.

You recognize that, yes, you're in the traffic jam; you're driving bumper-
to-bumper. You relax into it and surrender the fight. With the negativity
neutralized, your inner world expands and you create space for
possibility: "Now, what can you do with this situation?" You might listen
to music, call a friend (hands-free, of course) or listen to an audio book,
or you might just enjoy the silence. You've got options.

Isn't it amazing? Self-compassion transforms a moment of suffering
and turns it into a moment of love, connection, support, and presence.
Even when our circumstances don't change, our orientation to them can.
Out of stress and frustration come acceptance and peace.

**With self-compassion, we become part of our solution rather
than amplifying our problem.**

THE GUEST HOUSE

This being human is a guest house.
Every morning a new arrival.

A joy, a depression, a meanness,
some momentary awareness comes
as an unexpected visitor.

Welcome and entertain them all!
Even if they're a crowd of sorrows,
who violently sweep your house
empty of its furniture,
still, treat each guest honorably.
He may be clearing you out
for some new delight.

The dark thought, the shame, the malice,
meet them at the door laughing
and invite them in.

Be grateful for whoever comes,
because each has been sent
as a guide from beyond.

Rumi

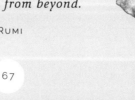

LEARNING THE SKILL

Most of us, unfortunately, do not grow up learning how to be kind to ourselves. Instead, we become quite familiar with a critical, even cruel voice in our head that tells us that some part of us is inept, flawed. Happily, the ACT practice is a learnable skill, and self-compassion is a natural ability that we all possess. Best of all, ACT and self-compassion are antidotes to the negative voice that keeps you stuck in resistance.

Self-compassion may be a creative process, but it is not a mystery. The ACT practice is a framework for harnessing compassion. It activates the care circuits in your brain so that the suffering parts of you will feel cared for and less alone. You soothe yourself. **As self-compassion feels more and more natural, you will begin to trust that you can be on your own side.**

While ACT is a powerful practice for reducing resistance, there are other ways to activate this new, gentler experience. For example, we can imagine receiving compassion from, and giving it to, other people, a technique that proved helpful with my patient Duncan.

Neuroscientist
Richard Davidson observes
that self-compassion is one
of the most powerful agents
of brain change known
to science.

Duncan came to see me after his wife, Lorraine, asked him for a divorce. He was shattered by this and begged her to go with him to therapy. She said that there was no point because she was absolutely done with the marriage. She had already had a meeting with a lawyer and she told Duncan that he needed to accept what was happening.

When I sat with Duncan the first time, he was resisting the divorce with all his might. He told me of ways he could win her back, and he couldn't believe that she meant what she was saying. His recipe for suffering was rejecting the truth of what was happening, and he was putting a lot of energy into his resistance.

Although Duncan and Lorraine, both in their mid-50s, had been married for 11 years, they had no children together. It was a second marriage for both and they lived in what had originally been Lorraine's house. According to Duncan, Lorraine had asked him to move out but, he had refused.

I listened to Duncan's distress. "I know that we didn't have a marriage made in heaven, but I never thought that she would pull the plug. I really didn't see this coming." Yet he had suspected that Lorraine was having an affair, and he had even had a brief affair himself five years previously.

As the days turned into weeks, Duncan's resistance continued. He still refused to move out, despite Lorraine's multiple requests, and he wasn't cooperating with the legal proceedings. A part of me wanted to say to him, "You need to accept what's happening!" I had a picture in my mind's eye of the singer/actor Cher, in the 1987 movie *Moonstruck*, slapping Nicolas Cage across the face and saying, "Snap out of it" after he told her the unwelcome news that he loved her.

Instead I said, "This is so hard for you, so crushingly painful to realize that you're married to someone who doesn't want to be married to you." Duncan got tears in his eyes. He looked down and acknowledged his sadness and his shame. "I've amounted to nothing; I'm broken by this", he said.

Duncan had taken the first step in the ACT practice of owning the truth of his inner experience, acknowledging it and naming it. I took Duncan to the next step by saying, "This is so excruciating. You are not alone in your sadness. You are part of a web of humanity that knows this kind of pain, of thousands of people who are also told by their partner that they want out."

Compassion, in general, wasn't part of Duncan's lexicon. He had grown up in a tough neighborhood where weakness was exploited and vulnerability was ridiculed. Anything smacking of tenderness was highly suspect. Opening up, as he was, already felt strange and unsafe. But as I talked kindly to him in that moment, he was able to take it in.

I continued, "Duncan, you're going to get through this."

He breathed, sighed and said, "But if I agree to this divorce, I'll have to admit what a failure I am. I am utterly worthless as a man, and I will be all alone."

I asked if he would be willing to try a visualization in both receiving and giving compassion. He had previously told me that practicing self-compassion sounded weak, as if he were letting himself off the hook or treating himself like a baby. But he said he was willing to try this exercise.

PRIMING THE PUMP OF COMPASSION: A VISUALIZATION

If direct self-compassion feels too difficult at first, it's helpful to experiment with the experience of "receiving compassion" from someone else, and/or the experience of "sending compassion" to someone else.

I asked Duncan to close his eyes and see if he could recall the image of a person or animal from whom he had previously felt some tenderness. He came upon the memory of his grandmother, who had loved him and offered relief from the chaos in his home. As he imagined her in front of him, smiling with love, he visibly relaxed. He spent some time here, letting himself imagine being with her, baking cookies, laughing together. He breathed in her love for him and was able to feel her compassion.

The instruction for the next visualization was to recall the image of a person or an animal toward whom *he* could direct uncomplicated and tender love. Smiling, he came upon the memory of his childhood dog. I asked him to imagine sending loving energy to that furry companion. Duncan's face softened and his breathing slowed. I invited him to spend a few minutes each day engaged in both visualizations.

The next week, Duncan was curious about ACT. I helped him craft these simple ACT sentences: **Acknowledge**—"Duncan, you are in pain." **Connect**—"Duncan, you are in the company of others who are forced into divorce." **Talk kindly**—"Duncan, you're going to be okay. You've been through hard stuff before." He agreed to spend a few minutes each day with these self-tailored ACT phrases. It was just a beginning for Duncan, but it would lead to a bigger shift. His moments of pain were an opportunity: they could also be his moments of self-consolation.

> **"*His moments of pain were an opportunity.*"**

BEGINNING TO HEAL

The next week, Duncan told me that he was going to stop his opposition to the divorce. *Wow*, I thought. While this was sad for Duncan, it was also emotionally freeing. For the first time in weeks, his anger and resistance were gone. He could begin to heal.

So what happened for Duncan? A few things. First of all, he was at peace. Even in his grief, his internal battle was over. Second, by becoming his own friend, he felt less alone and more courageous. Third, by embracing his own sadness he was open to receiving consolation and compassion from others. That's the irony of self-compassion: instead of making you weaker, it makes you stronger, more receptive, and more resilient. You're able to face the truth of something hard because you are supporting yourself. There is a subtle shift from focusing on pain to feeling supported, and this, in itself, is healing.

Duncan's self-compassion also provided him with a feeling that he would be okay in the future. By dissolving his inner opposition and relaxing the fight, he could flow forward. Even from the place of deep sadness, his world felt more expansive and he could glimpse possibility.

About a year after our final session, I heard from Duncan. He called to let me know how things had turned out. I only see a portion of any client's journey, and I am always happy to hear about how the story continued. He let me know that after he had moved out from Lorraine's home, they had officially divorced. He had taken up running as a new hobby and, through a local running club, he had met a new woman. He wanted to thank me for teaching him about both self-compassion and acceptance. He had a lot less resistance in his life now and a lot more peace. He was hoping that the combination would bode well for his new relationship. I suspect it will.

IT'S ALL ABOUT YOU

Acceptance is about turning toward yourself first, with an embrace, and *then* turning toward life with an open heart. Self-compassion, in essence, is a profound act of acceptance. When you start with you, with soothing yourself, you are set up to accept other people and other circumstances. But it all starts with learning how to be your own best friend.

POWER TOOLS

PRIMARY TOOL: ACT PRACTICE

This core practice is vital for developing the skill of self-compassion. You will see it used consistently throughout the book as a portal to acceptance. Everything from minor annoyances to major pain will offer you the opportunity to practice this skill.

Acknowledge your pain and your suffering.

Connect to all beings who also experience pain and suffering.

Talk kindly to yourself.

When using this practice, don't forget to talk to yourself in the second person. For example, "Oh [your name], I see that this is hard for you. You're not the only person to feel this way. You're going to be fine, honey. It's okay." Be intentional about using a warm and soothing tone, which will amplify the impact.

Know that you have the ability to soothe and comfort yourself. Research shows that using a physical gesture of tenderness further activates the care circuit of the brain and intensifies the feeling of being supported. Add one or more of the following self-compassion gestures, according to which feels the most soothing to you at the time:

A self-hug

Rubbing your arms

Crossing your hands over your chest and tapping right and left, alternating

One hand on the center of your chest, and one hand on your belly

One hand holding your other hand, and using your thumb to rub your wrist

One hand on your forehead, and the other hand on the back of your head

Hands cupping your face by cradling your cheeks

One or both hands on your heart

One hand on your sternum (breastbone)

BONUS TOOL:
IMAGINING "RECEIVING COMPASSION" EXERCISE

Close your eyes and imagine a loving person, animal, or spiritual figure who can offer you love, compassion, and acceptance. See yourself through the eyes of this being. Some examples of loving figures that you might choose are Mother Theresa, Mary, Krishna, Jesus, Buddha, the Buddhist goddess Kwan Yin, your grandparent, a coach, or your first pet. Visualize them seeing you with loving eyes, speaking to you with a compassionate voice. Visualize them sending you warmth, love, and compassion, even a hug. Put on their "glasses" and see yourself as they might see you.

How does this feel within your own body? Breathe deeply.

BONUS TOOL:
IMAGINING "SENDING COMPASSION" EXERCISE

Close your eyes and imagine yourself offering compassion to a person or an animal in need. It could be a child or someone you knew in the past, whether still on this planet or not. You could picture a small kitten or puppy who looks lost, wet, afraid. Imagine sending them warmth, love, compassion, and tenderness.

How do you feel when you see this being? What tenderness can you communicate to them? How do you want to provide comfort? Imagine yourself offering a hug, refreshment, a kindness. How does this feel within your own body? Breathe deeply.

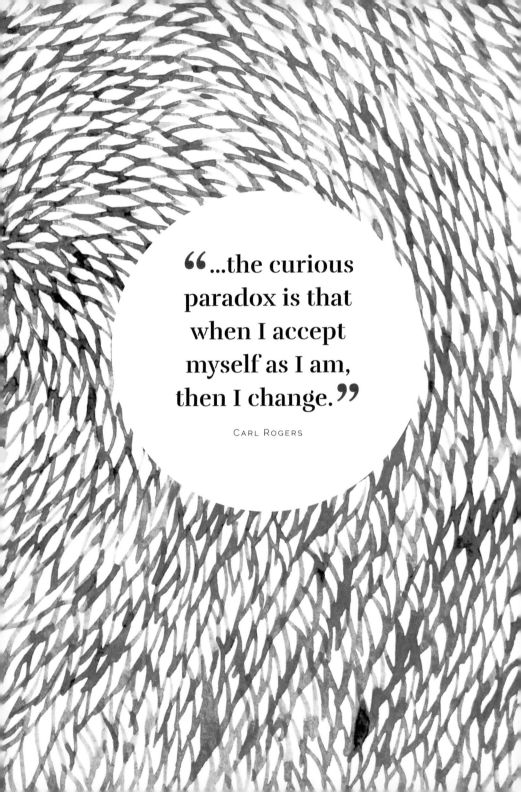

66 ...the curious paradox is that when I accept myself as I am, then I change. 99

CARL ROGERS

3

ACCEPTING YOURSELF

When Claude Anshin Thomas was 18 years old, he volunteered to fight in the Vietnam War. He was in active combat and won many distinctions, including a Purple Heart for valor. After the war, however, he was tormented. Suffering from post-traumatic stress disorder, he began using drugs and alcohol to numb his pain. He felt worthless, guilty, and lost. He hated himself for all the destruction he had caused in the war.

Several years later, on a retreat in search of healing and inner peace, he met Thich Nhat Hahn, a Vietnamese monk who taught Claude about compassion and acceptance. Hahn invited Claude to his monastery retreat center, called Plum Village, in France. There, Claude was placed in Lower Hamlet, a part of the center with a number of Vietnamese people. He felt nervous, fearful, and unsure of whether he would be accepted by the very group of people who had been his enemy. So he went into the woods, about a quarter mile from the community, and put up a tent. Around the perimeter of the tent he set up booby traps. Even after all this time, he still couldn't be sure who was his enemy and who was his friend.

In his autobiography, *At Hell's Gate*, Claude describes how he was changed by the experience of being unconditionally accepted. He notes that, when he told Sister Chan Khong about the fact that he had set booby traps around his tent, she was completely accepting of his need to do so. She let him know that, if he needed that protection, that was fine. And when he was ready to remove them, that would be fine too. He had never experienced that level of unconditional acceptance before.

The Vietnamese community loved Claude and assisted him in his healing. They accepted his past and accepted him, just as he was. Acceptance played a vital part in Claude's healing process. Because he felt so held and embraced by the Vietnamese people, he was able to internalize their acceptance, which led to his own self-acceptance. Now, many years later, he is a Zen Buddhist monk himself.

THE HEALING POWER OF BEING ACCEPTED

One of the primary reasons that good psychotherapy is such a powerful healing process for people is because the therapist offers the client an environment of unconditional acceptance. As with Claude's Vietnamese friends, the therapeutic relationship itself becomes a vehicle for acceptance and healing.

Once a client told me, "Well, now you've heard all my dirt. Are you going to fire me?" It was a poignant moment for her to hear that I saw her secrets and vulnerabilities not as dirt but as important parts of her rich life experience, and also that I was there for her no matter what she told me. In many ways, the psychotherapy office is a modern-day confessional. I routinely hear things that my clients are afraid to tell anyone else. I hold their secrets in a safe "container" and let my clients know that I accept what they feel and who they are. For many people, as for Claude Anshin Thomas, the act of being accepted by another stimulates an internal transformation of self-acceptance.

" *You hold the key within yourself.* **"**

The good news is that you don't need therapy or a Zen retreat center to find self-acceptance. You hold the key within yourself. The clients in my office actually experience self-acceptance on their own—I have merely planted the seed. As you read this book, you, too, are planting the seed for a whole new way of being with yourself. You can learn to provide yourself with comfort, understanding and acceptance. You can *learn* how to do it—from you, for you.

A good place to start is by accepting your feelings in any given moment.

GETTING STARTED

Frank blustered into my office, sat down forcefully and blurted out, "My problem is these damn tears. I cry every single day and I need to stop. I hate this. You have to help me stop these tears."

Frank was an 87-year-old man who had been coming to see me, off and on, for 7 years since the death of his beloved wife, Charlene. They had shared a truly epic love—a big, three-decade romance that rivaled the soul mates of Hollywood movies and Italian operas. He was bereft without her.

Frank and Charlene had met in midlife. Once they had found each other, they were inseparable. Since Charlene was eight years his junior, Frank had been certain that she would outlive him. When Charlene died quickly after being given a stage four cancer diagnosis, it was a shock to everyone.

I never got to meet Charlene, of course, but I felt as if I knew her. Frank shared story after story about her generous nature and her kind and loving countenance. Her love had made him a better man.

During our sessions, I normalized his grieving experience, shared in his sorrow, and encouraged him to know that his and Charlene's great love was part of him, always. Just because she was no longer on the planet didn't mean that their relationship was over. Quite the contrary, she was very much with him every minute of every day.

Frank re-engaged with life, even though he was heartbroken. He continued to travel, to sail his boat, and to spend time with his many cherished children and grandchildren. But each time he came to see me for a session, he would shake his head and say, "Will I ever get over losing Charlene?" And I would say, "You don't get over losing someone you love. You live with the vast loss and with the vast love every day."

This particular morning, Frank was finding his battle with his emotions overwhelming, and he implored me to help him get rid of his daily tears. The art of acceptance always begins with acknowledging the truth of your experience. I said gently, employing the ACT soliloquy (see Chapter 2), "**[Acknowledge]** Frank, you don't like your tears. You are suffering so much with your loss and with your expression of that loss. **[Connect]** You are grieving, like so many millions of people have throughout all of human history. **[Talk kindly]** Frank, you are living with a huge loss, and you're going to be okay. Your tears bear witness to yourself and to others about how a pure and generous love is a great blessing on this earth. Your tears reflect your love for Charlene, bringing you closer to her."

He looked a bit sheepish then and said, "Well, I never thought about my tears quite like that. I guess they're okay." His resistance was loosening.

The next time I saw Frank, he told me that he was not fighting the tears any more. He welcomed them as a sign of his connection to Charlene. And he was far gentler with his own sorrow, realizing that he was a man who had borne a great loss, but only because he had known—and still knew—a great love.

A CULTURAL PANDEMIC OF SELF-HATRED

Often we don't just hate our feelings and our symptoms, but hate our very selves. In 1990, a conference was held in Dharamsala, India, in which Western philosophers, psychologists, scientists, and meditators conversed with a learned Buddhist monk about matters of the heart and soul. During a question-and-answer period, one meditation teacher, Sharon Salzberg, asked the monk, "What do you think about self-hatred?" The monk looked startled and conferred with his translator, asking again and again for a translation that he could understand.

Finally, he turned back to Sharon, tilted his head and said in English, "Self-hatred? What is that?"

The attendees at the conference went on to explain that self-hatred was a common experience among people in the West, for people of all walks of life. The monk was genuinely curious about what he considered such a strange and unnecessary phenomenon. At the end of their discussion, he said, "I thought I had a very good acquaintance with the mind, but now I feel quite ignorant. I find this very, very strange."

Most people in Western culture have experienced some version of "self-hatred". As it turns out, our brains have a negativity bias, a wired-in, evolution-based tendency to scan for, notice and remember dangerous characteristics of our environment. This feature helped our ancestors survive. However, the individualism and competitiveness of Western cultures have turned the spotlight of negativity inward, creating an epidemic of self-loathing.

For many, the bias toward the negative creates a harsh inner critic. Moment by moment this voice whispers, *You're not good enough* or *Who do you think you are, loser?* or *You're not smart enough* or *Everyone knows that you're faking it.* Virtually everyone has experienced some version of this critical self. Its voice ranges from subtle to shockingly loud, shaming, undermining and belittling.

If you are like most people, of any age, education, wealth, or gender, you will have experienced the mistaken yet dark fear that you are not enough. The irony is that even though this is a common experience, **each of us feels that we are alone in our self-criticism.**

I can visualize a montage of people sitting across from me on the therapy couch in my office—year after year, decades even—telling me a version of the same story: "I am not enough". I can see a thin 40-year-old woman telling me that she isn't thin enough and a 60-year-old woman complaining that she isn't young enough. I remember the kind old man telling me that he is an idiot. I see the attractive heavy woman telling me that she hates her body, and the smart young man revealing that he can't look at himself in the mirror without flinching.

Tara Brach, spiritual teacher and author of *Radical Acceptance*, calls this self-critique "the trance of unworthiness". Each of us has a tendency to believe that we are unworthy—not likable, not attractive, not lovable, not smart, not good enough. Tara teaches that most of us live under the false assumption that there is something dreadfully wrong with us, something shameful about us and, as a result, we can be vicious and unmerciful with ourselves.

CHANGING YOUR RELATIONSHIP TO YOU

In the playful 2018 comedy film *I Feel Pretty*, Amy Schumer plays the role of Renee, a plain-looking, insecure young woman filled with self-loathing. Her only wish is to be beautiful, which she thinks will be the magical entrance into a happy life. After hitting her head during an exercise class, she suddenly believes herself to be thin and gorgeous (even though her appearance remains the same). As a result of her changed perception, her whole world changes. Her ensuing self-confidence and way of being in the world cause others to respond to her infectious enthusiasm.

By the end of the film, Renee snaps back to her "real" self. At first, she is horrified that she is no longer "beautiful". But then she comes to discover that she had never really changed at all, at least not physically. But she also realizes that, when she believed she was supermodel-beautiful, she acted with a confidence that, in fact, made her extremely attractive to others. She sees that beauty is about loving herself, accepting herself "as is" and being proud to be Renee. It is not about her externals. Her beauty is actually inside out. She thus realizes the power—and allure—of self-acceptance.

This charming film offers a powerful message, that "self-love is a commanding force for change". This may seem paradoxical and, in fact, it is. It's not that you should accept yourself so that you can change, but rather that in accepting yourself you create the space for change.

While Renee became self-confident by believing she was gorgeous, Leia Immanuel became self-confident by exposing what is traditionally not gorgeous. Leia is a teenage social media celebrity who has gained over 100,000 followers after posting selfies of her acne. She decided to share the "ugly" parts of her body and, as a result, touched a nerve among teenagers worldwide. Self-acceptance came from sharing the no-makeup truth and celebrating that which is usually hidden. Beauty is not just in the eye of the beholder, but also in the eye of those who are beheld.

Self-compassion is about allowing one part of yourself to offer loving kindness to another part—one that is inflicting judgement and negativity, however misguided. Self-compassion does not mean getting rid of, or changing, this part (even though change may come), but rather giving it attention. When working with your self-judgemental parts, the ACT practice provides a gentle way of being with yourself that allows your higher self to take things to a different level.

As you offer yourself compassion, the ACT practice might sound like this: **Acknowledge**—"That's a mean thought. It's painful to be so harshly judged. You're really suffering with this." **Connect**—"You're not the only one to think this way. We're all wired for negative thinking. Not feeling good enough is a common experience." **Talk kindly**—"You are doing the best you can. You are okay just as you are. You are special."

The ACT practice softens inner resistance, allowing all aspects of yourself to come to terms with your reality. Practiced often, self-compassion will become a habit, actually rewiring your brain for inner peace and creating new neural pathways for self-love.

**❝If anything is sacred
the human body is sacred.❞**

WALT WHITMAN

PUTTING IT INTO PRACTICE

Susanna is a 42-year-old woman who has struggled with her weight for her whole life. When she first came to see me, she was battling depression. She found it hard to work, hard to parent, hard even to get out of bed.

Susanna wanted to lose 23kg (50lb). She was certain that if she did so, she could love herself and build a better life. However, she had tried different weight-loss programs and nothing worked. She hated herself all the more because she couldn't stick with a diet.

The more she judged herself, the more she ate—and then beat herself up about her eating. You can imagine how a person who hates herself is likely to behave in self-destructive ways to punish herself. Susanna's resistance created the momentum for a downward spiral of hopelessness and suffering that was now creating resistance in all aspects of her life.

At the core of all this resistance, Susanna was tired of her lifelong battle with herself. She wanted to feel lovable and at peace. As with the path to any destination, we must start where we are. For Susanna, the starting point was her very real feeling of self-disgust. Using the ACT self-compassion practice, Susanna began by noticing and honoring her pain and suffering. Her dialogue with herself went something like this:

Acknowledge—"Susanna, I notice that you feel disgusted when you touch your stomach. Ugh, it's so hard when you hate your body and wish it were different than it is." **Connect**—"You're not alone in feeling badly about your body. Loads of women suffer so much with their weight." **Talk kindly**—"You deserve to be happy. I am here for you. You can be open to feeling differently. Maybe there's another way. Susanna, I love you just the way you are. You are more than your weight."

As Susanna began this daily internal dialogue, some spaciousness opened in her attitude toward herself. There was room for a gentle shift in perspective, an alchemy of emotions as she moved from self-attack to self-support, from feeling bad to feeling better. Simultaneously, we worked on her ability to be grateful to her body for all the ways that it served her—her legs allowing her to walk in the world; her eyes allowing her to see; her hands granting her the ability to type; the miraculous way that a cut healed on her arm. She started to see her body as a perfectly designed, useful, even miraculous vessel.

Over time, Susanna shifted. After repeatedly validating her own pain, connecting to the universality of her experience and talking kindly to herself, she accepted where she was and experienced greater inner peace. When she saw herself differently, she started to conduct her life differently. As you can imagine, a person who dwells in self-love starts to treat herself with reverence and thoughtful nourishment. The atmosphere of her life slowly changed.

Self-compassion and acceptance are interwoven creative processes that take time and build on themselves. Just as you don't eat one meal and think, *Great, I'm full forever*, and you don't exercise one day and think, *Yay, I'm fit for life*, you also don't simply say one kind word to yourself and expect negative thinking to vanish. The practice of self-compassion as the key to acceptance is a habit that needs revisiting over and over again. It's not just a new way to view yourself, but a new way of *being* with yourself.

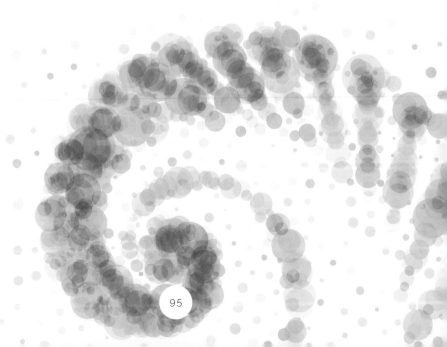

LITTLE AND OFTEN

As we know from neuroscience, the brain changes in response to repetition. Research into neuroplasticity tells us that the brain has the capacity to change throughout an individual's life, and that repetition is the basis for that change. Another way to approach changing your brain is to ask yourself the question, "What do I want to get really good at?" For example, if you repeat the habit of critical self-talk, you become a master of self-loathing and, if you repeat the habit of angry responses, you get really good at aggression—but wouldn't it be nicer to get really good at self-compassion?

Shauna Shapiro, a psychology professor who, in 2017, gave a popular TEDx talk on "The Power of Mindfulness", reframes neuroplasticity as "what you practise grows stronger". Shauna wanted to develop the habit of loving herself. She began small, with the new habit of saying to herself in the morning, "Good morning, Shauna, I hope you have a great day". And as she strengthened the habit of kindness, she added the statement "I love you, Shauna" each morning. She reported that it felt awkward at first, but over time she began to accept and absorb it. Soon she realized that she felt happier and more satisfied with her life. Because what you practice grows stronger, when you practice the art of self-acceptance via the vehicle of self-compassion, you will start to absorb acceptance into your very core.

* Accepting yourself *does not* mean that you stop striving to improve.

* Accepting yourself *does* mean that you love yourself just as you are.

MANY PARTS MAKE UP A WHOLE

What if you still believe that you're basically unlovable—or at least that certain aspects of you are? What if you've done something bad in your past? The present is always marked by past experiences, just as the growth rings of a tree are contained within its bark. Each year of a tree's growth moves outward from its core in concentric circles. Although some rings reflect years of drought or floods or a long cold winter, each ring is an aspect of the tree as a whole, supporting its height with increasing strength year after year. Like tree rings, all of our past selves and experiences are contained within us. When we come to accept each aspect as a crucial part of our present self, we feel strengthened and whole.

Remember Claude who became self-accepting once he felt accepted by the Vietnamese people? Claude had to wrestle with the fact that he had killed innocent people. He had to accept that, yes, he was a soldier as well as a recovering drug addict. But he was also a father, a son, a little boy, a guitar player, and a spiritual seeker. He was all these selves. When he was able to accept and integrate these parts into his whole self, he experienced the strength to heal. He said, "As I welcome all of these elements of myself into the present moment, I am able to participate more fully in my life...I would rather not have killed, but I have killed. And to reject that is to reject myself and the reality of my actions."

Like tree rings, all of our past selves and experiences are contained within us.

COMMUNICATING WITH OUR MANY PARTS

We are all made up of many aspects, many facets, many parts—perhaps a self-critical part, a judgemental part, an unkind part, a kind part, a hurt child, a wise elder, a caring soul, a selfish brat, a selfless angel. Richard C. Schwartz, the founder of Internal Family Systems (see page 59), explains that our inner world can be understood as being made up of multiple parts and that each of us can learn to understand ourselves when we learn to communicate with our parts. His premise is that all of your disparate parts are doing the best they can on your behalf to keep you safe...even the parts that appear to be hurting you.

In Schwartz's view of the self, every part wants to be accepted, understood, and appreciated. Thus, the goal isn't to eliminate parts of you, but rather to understand and embrace each and every one of them. Sometimes this means asking a part to step back. For example, the voice of a highly critical part might be trying to protect you from getting hurt. The part thinks if it keeps you small, you'll play safe and not take any emotional risks, thereby avoiding failure. While many of our parts had a crucial function in navigating hard times in childhood, often they are no longer needed in adult life. So, you can say to that part, "I've got this. You don't need to worry or try to protect me. I'll be okay no matter what, so you can relax and take some time off."

Rick was a 48-year-old man who was struggling with impulsive anger when we met. He had never been to therapy before and even now was extremely sceptical about the process. But his boss had threatened to fire him if he didn't get help with anger management. And so, under duress, he came to see me.

Rick wasn't particularly interested in self-compassion and thought it sounded weak. He believed in "kicking his own ass" if he was feeling emotional or angry. He was, however, willing to try mindfulness meditation because he thought it sounded scientific. After about a month of working together and becoming more comfortable with getting in touch with his inner world, he began to witness and thus separate a bit from his "angry thoughts".

When I introduced the idea of "parts" of self, Rick understood. He intuitively knew that he had an angry part, a scared part, a loving father-to-his-daughter part, a kind husband part, a judgemental part. But, of course, it was the angry part that so often had the microphone in his head.

One day, he was willing to close his eyes and let me guide him through a visualization. I asked for all of his "parts" to come together in a sort of group meeting. He selected the image of a table in a conference room as a gathering place for them. One by one, we invited the different parts to the table and Rick described who they were and what purpose they served in his life.

"The angry part doesn't want to sit at the table. He's super pissed off", said Rick, as his breathing started to pick up.

"How old is that part?" I asked gently.

"He's about eight years old", Rick answered softly.

"Can you tell that part that it's okay for him to be wherever he feels comfortable," I prompted, "and that he'll be safe?"

Rick, with his eyes still closed, had tears running down his cheeks. "That's just it", he said. "That little guy never feels safe."

The session unfolded with Rick's adult loving part comforting the young angry part, the eight-year-old boy, within himself. This young boy had, in fact, been abused by his alcoholic mother, thus quickly learning that the world wasn't particularly safe. It was a powerful breakthrough session.

After that, Rick was more open to the idea of self-compassion as a means of comforting himself. He could understand it as "one part of himself being nice to another". His anger began to dissolve as he internalized that he was basically safe in the world and could be his own best friend. As a result, he became a less reactive and much nicer employee at work.

KICK IT UP A NOTCH

Accepting yourself is an ever-changing process, a unique relationship with you. You can experience this developing relationship anywhere along a spectrum of enthusiasm—from a polite nod to a friendly handshake to a loving embrace. One way to move to the next level, intensifying the process from "benign allowing" to "extreme self-love", is to open yourself to a spiritual shift.

Experiment with seeing yourself as a "beloved" part of a greater whole. You are here at this moment in human history, a combination of DNA never to be repeated. You are as unique as a snowflake, irreplaceable. There has never been, and never will be again, a *you* exactly as *you* are now. You are special, sacred—and beloved as a vital being in the web of nature at this very moment in time.

This shift in perspective is in essence a spiritual experience. As you start to identify as a spiritual entity in a human body, you experience being part of something that is greater than yourself, a higher power, a greater spirit, something more. Whether you call this higher power Mother Nature, God, Spirit, Dharma, Allah, the Universe, the Greater Good, or no name at all, the experience of being divinely accepted and beloved can give new meaning to your life.

I invite you to investigate the path of *loving* and accepting yourself as a beloved part of all things sacred.

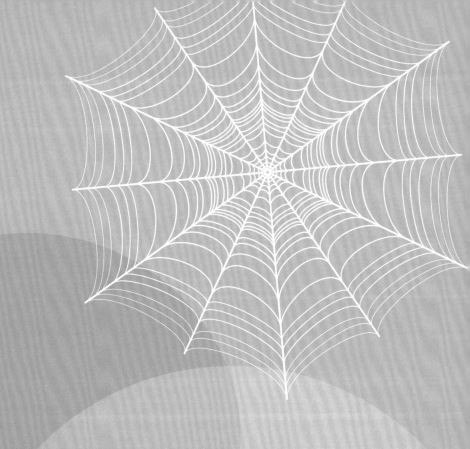

Remember, the you of today is different from the you of yesterday (your very cells completely replace themselves over a period of seven to ten years). And the you of today is also different from your future self. I suspect that your future self will thank you for the journey toward self-acceptance that you make, beginning today.

Once you strengthen the "muscle" of self-acceptance, you create a powerful momentum for accepting all things.

POWER TOOLS

PRIMARY TOOL: TIME TRAVEL EXERCISE

Look at a photograph of yourself when you were a child. Think about what it was like to be that child, to be you growing up. Close your eyes and see your current self in front of your child self. What would your current self like to say to that child self? Can you hug that child? Can you tell that child how things will be when they grow up? Does that child have anything to say to your current self? That child is a part of you, even today.

BONUS TOOL: MIRROR EXERCISE

When you are in front of a mirror in the morning and the evening, focus on your eyes. (Don't judge the wrinkles, moles, freckles.) Look into your eyes with a willingness to see beyond the surface. Say to yourself, "Hey there—you're amazing." Next see yourself, more deeply, as the you of today, full of life's experiences and lessons. Recognize that you are imperfect, that you are human—which is perfectly imperfect. See if you can feel some tenderness for you, the you who makes mistakes, who struggles, who tries, who loves. Say to yourself something like, "You're okay. You're you and you keep trying. You're a very special person."

BONUS TOOL: HEARTFELT MANTRA EXERCISE

1 Breathe deeply, low in your belly.

2 Put one or both hands over your heart and repeat the following mantra:

"Love is around you.

Love is within you.

You are One with Love."

3 Repeat and then repeat again.

**"Be kind,
for everyone you
meet is fighting
a hard battle."**

PLATO

4

ACCEPTING OTHERS

When I met my husband, Daniel, he ate raw meat. He was a carnivore of carnivores. Our mutual delight was grilling bacon cheeseburgers and slow-cooking pulled barbecue pork. Spicy western chili with rice was a winter Sunday staple. Together we roasted pork chops, noshed on beef stew, and snacked on steak tips (an East Coast staple). Our cuisine structured our traditions together and was the stuff of romantic memories.

And then Daniel became a vegetarian. He didn't ask me to follow suit, but it wasn't the same to dig into a plate of buffalo wings by myself. Our food choices now created a divide rather than the customary camaraderie. So I decided to become a vegetarian, too.

As a result, artisanal cheese boards and omelette stations became our mutual smorgasbord. New delights were discovered, like fondue for two, spice-crusted quiches, and Spanish frittatas. We fashioned aged-Cheddar tastings and creative inventions, such as egg, cheese, and peanut butter on biscuits.

Then Daniel became a vegan. Was there anything left to eat? Our flirtatious food fests had come to a screeching halt and I was sad. Really sad. Daniel was a new man with a new mission. The farm boy/hunter I had married now refused to eat any animal products. I was shocked and felt whiplashed by the thought that *you're not the man I married!*

Obviously, accepting a spouse's dietary metamorphosis is a relatively minor event compared with something big, such as your partner's infidelity. But for me, a similar emotional process of resistance ensued. Thoughts swirled in my head: *Don't change! I don't want this! Stop it! Let's go back to the way we were!*

Of course, over time, partners undergo a wide range of changes: "You had hair when I married you." "Well, you used to be a size 4." "You had low cholesterol when we met." "Well, you were an atheist then." Yes, we are changing all the time...in both welcome and unwelcome ways.

Unfortunately, we don't get to choose or control most changes, especially those of other people. And sometimes, defying the predictable ebb and flow of time, the very people we hope will change actually don't change.

How many young adults partner with the thought, *Oh he'll change... he'll drink less when we get married* (he doesn't)? Or *she'll change... she'll want to have children after a few years* (she doesn't). I'm reminded of the title of the 1996 Off-Broadway musical *I Love you, You're Perfect, Now Change.*

Here's the irony of change: you cannot depend on it absolutely even though it is inevitable! There are always people who we hope will change who don't, and others who we hope won't change who do.

SISTER AT THE FUNERAL

Judy came to see me before a family funeral. She wasn't close to her brother and hadn't actually seen him since he had moved to California a few years previously. But their father had died and now the families were gathering in Boston for a "celebration of life" service.

Judy was resentful toward her brother. He hadn't participated in their father's end-of-life care and she wanted him to, first, apologize for what he didn't do; second, thank her for what she had done; and, last, take some responsibility by handling all of the memorial arrangements.

I listened to Judy's concerns, her feelings, her lifetime grudge that the fun, wild brother had "checked out" and done his own thing while she, the dutiful daughter, had cared for their father for years.

"But if John could step up—just this once. I have to make him do this!" Judy protested.

Judy's grief was compounded by her desire for her brother to meet her expectations, even though her hopes were inconsistent with his usual behavior. She was grieving for her father and lamenting the reality that her brother wasn't the man she wanted him to be.

Judy was trying to change her brother in order to find closure and peace. But, of course, that was an exercise in futility. She couldn't change him, though she had tried through the years. The truth that Judy had yet to realize was that her very resistance to her brother was causing her distress. She wouldn't be able to find peace until she accepted her brother "as is", in his present condition, with all of his faults.

Her resistance to something she had no power to change was at the heart of her suffering. But the good news about acceptance is that you actually do have the power. You hold the key. While Judy didn't recognize this—not yet—she was very aware of her pain.

FIRST STEPS

At first I simply acknowledged Judy's resistance and taught her about self-compassion. Self-compassion was a new concept to her, as it is for so many of us. She was afraid that it would make her weak, not strong. It even made her feel a bit guilty, as if she didn't deserve it. Isn't it curious that we so easily offer compassion to others but when it comes to offering compassion to ourselves, we struggle?

Accepting that she was resistant to self-compassion, Judy started with the following self-dialogue based on the ACT practice (see Chapter 2): **Acknowledge**—"Judy, I see that you're struggling here. This feels awkward and uncomfortable...and a little stupid, actually." **Connect**—"Lots of people have issues with self-compassion." **Talk kindly**—"It can be hard to talk kindly to yourself but, well, you need some peace. You *deserve* some peace. It's okay. You're okay."

While it felt strange, Judy desperately wanted relief from the agony of resistance. She was committed to working with this practice. She continued to acknowledge her pain in the moment by connecting to others experiencing the common struggle and by talking kindly to herself. Soon she could say to herself: **Acknowledge**—"Judy, I see that you're really stressing out here. You want John to be different than he is and it's super frustrating for you." **Connect**—"You're not the first person to be disappointed by a sibling. Others know the same feeling." **Talk kindly**—"Honey, breathe. You're going to get through this."

When Judy saw me the week after her father's funeral, she reported that the weekend had been both a success and a failure. She hadn't been able to fully accept her brother. Over and over again she found herself falling back into the old trap of wishing he was different than he was. But she did succeed in accepting her resistance by acknowledging (with compassion) her own suffering. As she began to embrace self-acceptance as a personal creative process, she was surprised by how much less she suffered.

Judy had found victory in being kind to herself. Every time she started to get snagged by her annoyance toward John, she redirected her attention away from him and, instead, became gentle with her own experience. She shook her head as she acknowledged, "It could have been so much worse. I rolled my eyes a lot but I didn't yell at John or demand an apology." She pointed out that, even though he wasn't particularly nice to her, she was nice to herself. Judy no longer gave John power over her own feelings. Rather, she felt empowered by her new-found ability to honor and accept herself.

At some point in the future, Judy may move into alignment with John as he is, without wishing for him to change (thinking to herself, that's John being John). But for the moment she was able to align with her own experience as it was. And in that lay the seeds for change, within the deep expansiveness of self-compassion. **Accepting your own experience creates the gateway for accepting others.**

ACCEPTING THE PACKAGE DEAL

I once heard the phrase, "I like you because...but I love you despite..."
(from a Netflix movie called *Set It Up*). I didn't understand these words
at first because they sounded vaguely negative, more like "I love you
despite the fact that you leave the toilet seat up and are always late".
It sounded to me like a backhanded compliment.

On closer inspection, however, I noticed that the phrase is really about
unconditional love. "I love you even though...I love you with your pros
and your cons...I love you in spite of your mistakes and your foibles."
And don't we all have foibles? "I accept you as you are." We all long for
unconditional acceptance; it is a tremendous gift.

When my children were young, I used to tell them that I loved them no
matter what they did or ever could do—I would love them if they got
bad grades at school, if they told lies, if they moved far away, if they chose
careers that I didn't like, if they chose spouses I didn't like. I would love
them if they were drug addicts, thieves, or murderers. I really meant it.

While, of course, I didn't wish for any of these outcomes, I was sincere
in my desire to love them no matter what. But I didn't anticipate that
my eldest daughter, Hilary, would one day cause me to think, "I love you
even when you say you hate me and seem to have stopped loving me"!
But that's exactly what happened.

66 *We all long for unconditional acceptance; it is a tremendous gift.* **99**

TROUBLED TIMES

Hilary was 14 years old when I asked her father for a divorce. She was utterly devastated. She had always been a sensitive child, and having her world fall apart in her adolescence was a heavy burden for her to bear. Of course, I felt terrible...and guilty. It broke my heart that a choice that I was making to improve my life was doing exactly the opposite to hers.

Hilary's pain, however, quickly manifested as anger. Her rage was focused on me, her mother. For the next months and years, Hilary directed a vitriolic hatred toward me that was extremely painful for both of us. Even when you know *why* a hurt person is being hurtful—even when you can understand and forgive it—it is still quite agonizing to be on the receiving end of such anger.

Hilary alternately screamed at me and shunned me. She became a master at stonewalling, rolling her eyes, and criticizing me at every turn. The worst moment for me was when the school nurse called me after Hilary had hit her head during a gym class. When I arrived, she was resting on a bed and said loudly to the nurse, "I don't want *her* here." My own daughter's rejection of me was public and personal.

Finally, I went to a counselor myself since Hilary refused to go with me. I teared up as I described how my daughter despised me, how we had been close when she was little, how there didn't seem to be any solution.

This wise woman shook her head and said, "Oh honey, this is really painful. Don't the ones we love hurt us the most?" In a soothing voice she continued, "You are not alone in suffering anger from a teenager. Just accept her for today, that's all you have to do. You don't know how things will be different in the future. You're going to be okay. It's just for *today*."

As I left that session, feeling acknowledged and comforted, she added, "And be gentle with yourself. It's not easy, what you're going through."

I learned something about myself as a result of that experience. I learned that I could start small, that I only needed to accept someone or something one day at a time. And I learned that it was all right to be compassionate with myself first. Compassion for Hilary would follow.

My own ACT script sounded something like, "Ashley, this is so hard. You hate being rejected by this child who is so dear to you. It's heartbreaking for you. You're not the first parent to be hated by a child. You are a loving mother and you're going to get through this, one day at a time."

All these years later, happily, we found our way back to each other.

HURT PEOPLE HURT PEOPLE

When people are mired in anger, when they react defensively, they are actually feeling hurt or afraid. Haven't we all experienced the anger that protects our pain? Tara Brach, author of *Radical Acceptance*, describes the scenario of coming upon a dog in the woods that is snarling, growling, and barking at you. You recoil in fear and even anger at this aggressive beast. But then you notice that the dog's paw is caught in a trap. He is lashing out because he is in terrible pain. Your fear softens to compassion, concern. You may or may not be able to help this poor creature get free from the trap, but your perspective toward him has changed.

Whether it is you who is stuck in the anger of resistance or it is someone who is directing this anger toward you, pain is the common denominator. Both of you long for and deserve compassion.

Hurt people hurt people. That's how it goes. By virtue of being human, we are naturally prone to being hurt. It is a universal condition.

AN UNLIKELY TEACHER

When you remember that every single person you meet—of every age, in every country, in every culture—simply longs to be loved, when you see them as hurting, you start to have a more forgiving attitude. All humans long for happiness and are subject to pain and suffering. In this, we are all united. We are all students and teachers for each other.

Our unlikely teachers are those people in our lives who challenge us to learn about ourselves. Anyone can be your unlikely teacher: your annoying boss, your nasty ex-spouse, the driver who just cut you up, your children who didn't turn out the way you expected, your parents who didn't provide what you needed, your deceitful business partner.

"Be grateful to everyone" is a powerful Buddhist mantra, a training phrase for meditation. If someone in your life is challenging you (either because they won't accept you or because they make it hard for you to accept them), the challenge for you is to stop and see past their exterior, to see them as someone like you who has needs and desires and frailties. Since we are all connected in our humanity, when you practise self-compassion it will eventually spill into compassion for others.

Of course, this can feel difficult. That's all right. When it feels like too much to be grateful to your enemy, then gently go back to self-compassion and notice your resistance. Let yourself know that you are not alone in dealing with anger, frustration, or shame. You are okay just as you are. Before you can accept others, you must always begin by accepting your own feelings about that other person. **Self-compassion leads to self-acceptance. Self-acceptance leads to the acceptance of others.**

IMAGINING COMPASSION FROM ANOTHER

How does accepting others look in practice? Let's take the story of Samantha and Greg, two people divorcing and in pain. Samantha said she hated Greg because he was the one who betrayed her and abandoned her; he was the one who broke her heart. Greg seemed to hate Samantha, too, and was cruel and hostile to her. He always knew how to push her buttons.

Samantha came to see me while the divorce proceedings were in motion because she thought that she was going to lose her mind. I realized that I couldn't tell her to be grateful for Greg, or that he was her teacher. She wasn't ready to hear that. But I also knew that the only way for her to find peace was to accept that Greg was who he was.

In the beginning, Samantha was so triggered by Greg's demands and nasty emails and texts (she always responded with something even more nasty and demanding) that it was difficult for her to stop focusing on Greg and notice her own pain. Self-compassion felt too challenging to Samantha at first, so she started by imagining that she was receiving compassion from her grandfather. He had raised her and had been a rock in her life. Samantha could imagine him sitting beside her, drinking coffee and saying, "Hun, have a cup of cocoa with me. Just rest here till you feel better." Samantha imagined acknowledgement, connection, and kind words from him that soothed her and allowed her to align with her own feelings. So the compassion she imagined from her grandfather was followed by compassion from herself to herself.

As the weeks went by, every time she noticed anger at Greg, she simply imagined her grandfather and her wiser self offering compassion. Then she would relax, breathe, and smile. Eventually, she was able to see an email or text and simply think, "That's Greg being Greg". She stopped wishing that he would behave differently, which allowed her to refocus on her own reaction.

Over time, Samantha actually started to feel some compassion for Greg, noticing that he must be suffering if he was living with so much anger. This metamorphosis took time for Samantha, but the pain and hurt of feeling like a victim had motivated her. The path of acceptance (both of herself and of Greg) offered her a path to inner peace.

As her practice of acceptance advanced, she was able to thank Greg (in her mind) for teaching her not only about her own suffering but also about her own strength, her own patience, and her own resilience.

* Accepting others
does *not* mean that you
approve of their behavior.

* Accepting others
does mean that you allow
their humanity.

WISHING OTHERS WELL

When I was going through my own divorce over a decade ago, I went to a Buddhist center to learn more about meditation and was introduced to the loving-kindness practice known as the *metta bhavana*. It is a meditation of sending compassion not only to the self but to all beings. In the five progressive stages of this practice, I was instructed to direct loving-kindness and well wishes to:

1 Myself (as we did in Chapter 3)

2 A loved one (easy to do)

3 A stranger—someone you crossed paths with, like the cashier at the grocery store (fairly easy to do)

4 Someone you are in conflict with or you struggle with (sometimes extremely hard to do)

5 All beings (moving from your town to your country to your hemisphere to the whole world)

In each stage, I was instructed to say: "May you be happy, May you be healthy, May you be safe from harm, May you know peace."

This went fairly well until stage 4. *What was that fourth one again? Send loving kindness to someone you struggle with?* The obvious choice at the time was my ex-husband and I wasn't feeling the love.

But my wiser self knew that holding onto anger and resentment is like swallowing poison but hoping the other person will die. Or it's like holding onto a hot coal, ready to fling it at the other, while all the time it's burning your own hand.

In the beginning, I had to simply go through the motions of offering loving-kindness to my ex-husband. Even to imagine it felt awkward and forced at first. I added the ACT practice for me even as I did the loving-kindness practice for him. My inner dialogue went something like this: **Acknowledge**—"Ashley, it feels strange to wish him well right now when it's tense between us." **Connect**—"You know that lots of people have strained relationships with their exes." **Talk kindly**—"You can give this a try. He's a person, just like you, who wants to live a happy life. Go ahead, you can do it." Loving-kindness meditation—"May you be happy, May you be healthy, May you be safe from harm, May you know peace."

As I continued with *both* practices, I did start to feel actual compassion for him. And I experienced more and more freedom as a result.

KICK IT UP A NOTCH

Accepting a so-called "enemy" can feel challenging, but what about actually *forgiving* that person for a terrible deed they have done? That can feel like quite another project altogether. Forgiveness is taking acceptance to a new level.

A very public and powerful example of amazing forgiveness is the story of Mary Johnson, the founder of Death to Life, an organization that encourages forgiveness between families of victims and their murderers. In 1993, her only child, 20-year-old Laramiun, was murdered by Oshea, 16 years old at the time. Oshea spent 17 years in prison and Mary hated him at first. She was full of anger and bitterness.

One day she read a poem about a bereaved mother and the mother of the murderer, and Mary realized that they were both mothers in pain. She knew that her path to her own healing would come by forgiving Oshea. Forgiveness wasn't about agreement—she would always prefer to have her son back—but about healing and her own freedom from hate.

Mary went to see Oshea in prison and saw him simply as a person who had made a terrible mistake. When she hugged him, she says that the anger rose from the soles of her feet and left her, and that she has been free from hatred ever since. Later they became neighbors and friends, and now they work together to spread the good news of acceptance, forgiveness, and reconciliation.

Of course, forgiving your child's murderer is a pretty tall order. It may not be possible for everyone. But perhaps the deeper lesson here is that you and others—you and I—are one in our shared common humanity.

When you accept yourself, you learn to accept others. And when you accept others, you learn to accept yourself.

Marianne Williamson, a spiritual teacher about the principles found in the book *A Course in Miracles,* is fond of saying that we're all just spokes on a wheel. If you focus on the rim of the wheel, it seems that we are all very different from each other, very far apart. But if you focus on the hub of the wheel, you see that we are all the same—all from the same source.

Everyone you meet is born into this world and must die in this world. Everyone you meet wants to live in happiness and peace and to avoid pain and suffering. When you see another as an extension of yourself, as a person doing the best that they can just as you are (even if that is imperfectly), you begin to extend your self-compassion to compassion for all beings.

❝ *Forgiveness is taking acceptance to a new level.* ❞

POWER TOOLS

PRIMARY TOOL: GLASS HALF FULL

It can be challenging—deeply upsetting, in fact—when you love someone very much but you just don't like some aspect of them or particular thing that they do. This aspect may be minor, such as their haircut, clothing style, or sense of humor. But it could feel intense, perhaps rooted in your sense of concern or morality: you don't like their politics, their religion, their weight (too heavy, too thin), their health habits, their choice of career, where they live, their sexual orientation, their choice of partner/spouse. Sometimes a singular trait of a person you love can cause a chronic wedge between you.

Your loved one has their own path in this world just as you have yours. And in spite of your differences, you still love this person and want them in your life. This tool is about seeing your friend or loved one in a context larger than a single characteristic. Instead of focusing on what you don't like, focus on what you do like about this person. When you look to their positive traits, you find a way to alignment, to acceptance of them as they are. So, the next time you notice one of these irritating characteristics (which you absolutely cannot change or influence), attempt to see the glass half full.

1 Start with self-compassion. Notice that it's hard to have someone you love whom you wish you could change/help/improve. You feel helpless but you're open to feeling better about this. So...

2 Name three traits that you really love about that person.

3 Name two more behaviors that really touch you about them.

4 Now blow into the air and say, "I release you to your own path. I wish you peace and joy, health and happiness. May you find your way with ease and may you always feel loved."

BONUS TOOL: HO'OPONOPONO

Say the following sentences while imagining the person with whom you struggle. Ho'oponopono is a Hawaiian healing practice for reconciliation and forgiveness. Say the following words out loud or in your head. Even if you don't connect with the words, say them anyway with humility. They stimulate repentance, forgiveness, gratitude and love—four extremely powerful agents of change.

"I'm sorry.

Please forgive me.

Thank you.

I love you."

Using and contemplating these words as a mantra each and every day will open your heart and create emotional healing. You are putting an energetic course correction in motion to reset your relationship with life.

BONUS TOOL: JOURNAL REFLECTION

Reflect, in writing, on these prompts:

* "When I am stuck in my own resistance, I feel..."

* "When I want this person to be other than how they are, I feel..."

* "When I accept this person just as they are, I feel..."

* "Others are suffering and I know what it feels like to suffer. Therefore..."

* "What have I done for this person lately?"

* "What harm have I caused for this person lately?"

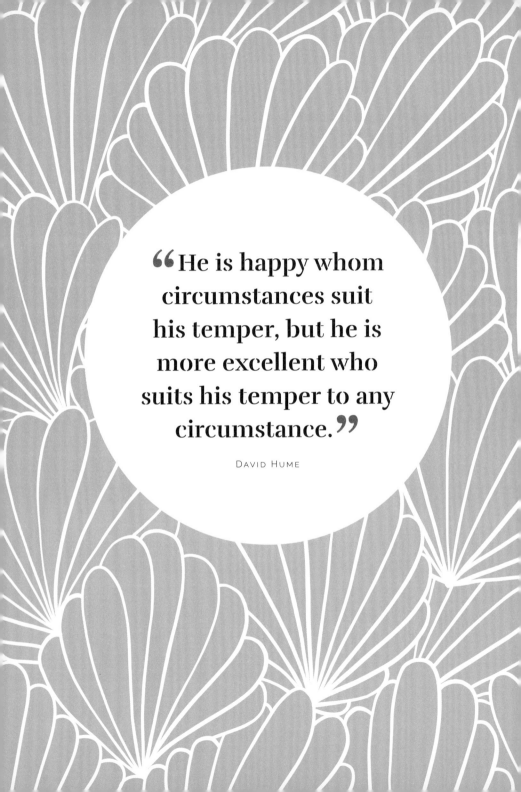

"He is happy whom circumstances suit his temper, but he is more excellent who suits his temper to any circumstance."

David Hume

5

ACCEPTING YOUR CIRCUMSTANCES

There are circumstances you can change and those you cannot. Either way, acceptance is the launching pad.

Eckhart Tolle, author of *The Power of Now*, talks about acceptance in an interview with Oprah Winfrey on one of her Super Soul Sunday conversations. Tolle tells Oprah that stress is caused by wanting something to be the way that it isn't. He instructs that we must always start by accepting the present moment exactly as it is. Only then can we determine if circumstances can be changed or not. As an example, Tolle says to imagine that you are stuck in mud. You may be angry about it and complain or cry. But you actually make it worse for yourself in this situation. He suggests that you look at the situation without labelling it. When you acknowledge "what is", you shift your consciousness and then you can decide what to do next.

In other words, it's the resistance itself that causes all sorts of trouble.

Resistance keeps you stuck. Very stuck.

* Accepting circumstances does *not* mean that you like what's happening.

* Accepting circumstances *does* mean that you work with what you've got.

UNAVOIDABLE CIRCUMSTANCES

Obviously, there are many circumstances that, once you accept them, you will choose to change. Leaving an abusive relationship, feeding a hungry person, quitting a smoking habit and fixing a flat tire are examples of positive change. But many, many circumstances are initially beyond our control and so cannot be changed.

Circumstances beyond our control are the most intolerable ones because they activate a sense of helplessness and frustration. These range from the mundane to the tragic:

Does your blood pressure rise as you read the list opposite? I'm sure you can add your own versions of annoying—and unavoidable— circumstances. They are simply a part of life. How you handle them, of course, is what makes the difference between misery and peacefulness. The question to ask yourself is, "How do I want to be with my unavoidable circumstances? Do I want the suffering of resistance or the peace of acceptance?" You hold the key to that answer.

Even when we cannot change circumstances, we can change our attitude toward, our orientation to, and our relationship with those unchangeable circumstances. Acceptance makes all the difference.

Your flight is delayed. • Your child is sick. • You've broken your tooth. • A boss or co-worker is being really annoying. • You're stuck in a traffic jam. • Your spouse asks for a divorce and you're shocked. • You discover that your partner has betrayed you. • You're told at work that you're being fired. • You get a shocking medical diagnosis. • Emergency surgery is necessary. • An unexpected bill arrives. • Your car breaks down. • Your computer dies. • Your eyesight is going. • You've injured your wrist. • You've slipped on black ice. • A car has hit you from behind. • Your dog ran away. • Your home has had a power cut. • The train is cancelled. • Your new love dumps you. • The cat throws up on your carpet. • Your work project deadline gets moved forward. • A hurricane has flooded your house.

MINIMAL RESISTANCE

Byron Katie, in her ground-breaking book *Loving What Is*, writes about dropping her resistance to the point where she goes with the flow of whatever circumstance presents itself, 100 percent of the time. Calling herself "a lover of reality", she teaches that your thoughts about your circumstances, not reality itself, are what cause your suffering. Change your thoughts and you change your relationship to your circumstances.

I once attended a workshop to hear Byron Katie speak about her Zen-like relationship with life. She told the crowd that it is possible to welcome news of any kind. Whether it is the impending birth of a grandchild or a cancer diagnosis, it is all the same—simply news. There need not be any resistance at all. Of course, most of us are not enlightened and we do often have strong reactions to new information. Byron Katie's lesson is not that we need to be nonreactive, but that acceptance is within our grasp.

While the overarching goal of acceptance is to align with the circumstances as they present themselves, aligning with our resistance always comes first. We have to first admit that we don't like being in the situation. **Be with your resistant feelings and thoughts, exactly as they are, and then healing will happen.**

GRIEF WORK

Our culture doesn't encourage the expression of pain. Over my three decades in the mental health field not much has changed in this respect. We tend to label stoicism as strength. We applaud pulling ourselves up by our own bootstraps. If people collapse in pain, we want to cajole them out of it. We offer platitudes and distractions—anything to avoid sitting with their pain or ours.

But when a person has suffering in their life, not acknowledging it (or even denying it) only makes their suffering worse. So how can we help a person in pain? The kindest, most powerful response is to simply and compassionately acknowledge it. This doesn't remove the pain, of course, but it lessens its severity because then the sufferer feels less alone. They feel accepted. You validate their experience and offer your presence. Over time, this supports their healing process.

This loving acknowledgement is exactly the process that you offer yourself with self-compassion. Let's say you resist something sad, like the death of a parent. Of course you are heartbroken. Self-compassion, as expressed through ACT (see Chapter 2), helps you feel validated and connected to others in your experience of loss. As you align with your own experience, you relax into it and start to heal. Alignment with feelings leads to alignment with circumstances. Let's see how that looks...

RITUALIZING THE PROCESS OF ACCEPTANCE

Jim and Veronica had wanted nothing more than a baby of their own. In fact, Veronica had been dreaming about having a large family since she was young. When she was a teenager and she babysat other people's children, she would think to herself, *One day I'll have a little girl like this and be a mother*. The thought thrilled her well into adulthood.

By the time she came to see me, Veronica was 41 and the couple had been trying unsuccessfully for more than a decade to have a child. Years of infertility specialists, enormous sums spent on medical procedures, and still no baby.

Why didn't they adopt a child? It wasn't part of her story. Veronica had been adamant that she wanted to give birth and feel a child grow within her own body. She didn't want just any baby—she wanted her baby. But now she had to let go of that dream.

Jim and Veronica were something of a medical mystery in that there was no explanation for their infertility. And yet something obviously wasn't working. When I met Veronica, she blamed her body. She blamed her husband. She blamed the universe. Although she was bitter and clearly stuck in resistance, Veronica was tired of being miserable. She wanted to look at other people's children and not feel jealous. She wanted to stop being angry with her husband. She wanted to enjoy her life and live in peace.

We started with her resistance, her suffering, her feelings of anger. And we added to that big doses of self-compassion. For Veronica, sending loving-kindness directly toward herself felt difficult, but we found what would prove helpful: to imagine herself receiving compassion from a spiritual figure. For her, the Virgin Mary was a symbol of love and tenderness in her life. Veronica identified with the Virgin Mary as a bereaved mother, someone who understood pain and grief. Veronica pictured herself kneeling in front of Mother Mary, hearing words of acknowledgement and kindness, and receiving compassion as a shining light upon her head.

Veronica was touched by her vision of Mary understanding her suffering, identifying with her pain. And as Veronica began to accept and absorb Mary's compassion for her, her own compassion for Mary arose. She imagined a circle of compassion and was eventually able to rest in the middle of it.

Self-acceptance opened Veronica to a shift. She stopped fighting her resistance to her circumstances and allowed herself to align with them. But alignment, at least at first, was a painful place. She needed to mourn the loss of her story, the loss of her hope, and there were many sessions of tears as she let herself feel her sorrow.

Veronica created two rituals to help her move forward. In her first ritual, her goal was to release the dream of having a biological child. She placed a daisy chain in a nearby lake, letting it drift away on its own current, off on its own path. Her second ritual was to honor the fact that she and Jim were a complete family, even though it was just the two of them. She chose two river stones, which she placed in her garden.

As Veronica gradually moved along the path of acceptance, she opened up to possibility. "And now?" I asked. "What might you do with your maternal energy?"

Veronica was inspired to create meaning out of her loss by taking action. She considered a few options, including being a foster mother, tutoring children in a nearby school or even just taking the opportunity to develop some of her own hobbies. In the end, she became a volunteer at the local animal shelter. She felt a call to use her caregiving energy to help animals in need. She also adopted two cats and gave them a loving home. Veronica and Jim were able to move forward with their lives together, rewriting a new story one day at a time.

Veronica's ACT practice ebbed and flowed over time, with self-talk ranging from "gentle soother" to "cheerleader". She was creative with herself. At times she needed to align with her sadness, and at other times she needed to give herself permission to move on. Self-compassion allows us to tune into ourselves and discern what we need and when. Do you need the proverbial cup of tea or a bit of a nudge? You get to decide.

FAIR WEATHER

The process of acceptance (moving from resistance to alignment to possibility—see Chapter 1) is the same whether the circumstance is tragic or mundane. It is valid for grief and valid for minor annoyances. But even minor inconveniences can feel major in the moment.

Arlene came to see me because she was suffering from what she thought was Seasonal Affective Disorder (SAD). For Arlene, she could feel her mood begin to slide downward with the change of clocks in the autumn. Then she slid further into a type of "hibernation"-induced depression that lasted until May. I knew how she felt since I have struggled to endure long, dark winters as well.

As I worked with her, self-compassion played a part in honoring her experience. But it also helped her align with her reality. Her self-talk became more motivational: "Come on Arlene, some fresh air today will do you good. It's okay if it's cold outside. Put on an extra sweater and move your body!"

Self-compassion is the key to aligning with resistance, and it also pivots you toward alignment with your circumstances. For Arlene, her self-talk boosted her confidence, helping her to feel supported and courageous.

IN SICKNESS AND IN HEALTH

It might seem like a big jump to go from discussing weather to cancer, but the process of acceptance is the same. In 2012, we received the news that my husband, Daniel, had colon cancer. When I heard, I burst into tears. I resisted the news with everything that I had—*This can't be. NOOOOOOO. We don't want this. We can't have this. I want it to be different. This isn't supposed to happen to us.*

And my agony didn't end with that bombshell. I landed in my resistance over and over and over again. I resisted when Daniel got the stint put into his chest. I resisted the nurse visits. I resisted when he lost weight. I resisted when he went into what I called "the valley"—the biweekly cycle of sickness so severe that he was incapacitated for days at a time.

When I say resisted, what I mean is that I continued to suffer. *I hate this. I hate this for Dan and I hate this for me. I hate cancer.* I don't want this in our lives. I was in battle mode, fighting it, wrestling it. The stress of my resistance affected my sleep, my mental health, and even my relationships (let's just say that I was not fun to be around).

66*Self-compassion guided me along the process of acceptance.***99**

And how did Daniel, the actual cancer patient, handle it? Like a Zen monk. There was no sense of being a victim, no reaction of *why me?* He let everything go and aligned with each moment exactly as it was. He didn't see cancer as the enemy, the battle to be fought. He wanted to heal and he wanted a "cure" and he wanted to live, definitely. But he did so with peaceful, nonviolent opposition. He was Gandhi to his cancer. He used modern Western medicine and then he surrendered. He took one day at a time with a peacefulness that I envied. Even all these many years later, cancer free, Daniel looks back on that time as being one of intentional surrender and serenity.

My alignment to his cancer, however, was hard-won and had to be realigned on a daily basis. Self-compassion was my friend as, over and over, I noted the struggle: **Acknowledge**—"Ashley, your resistance is making this worse for you." **Connect**—"Ashley, you are not alone. Cancer touches millions of people and their loved ones every year." **Talk kindly**—"This is how it is for today, and today you will be better off if you flow with this rather than against it. You go, woman! You can handle this."

Self-compassion guided me along the process of acceptance. Aligning with the reality of our circumstance allowed me to be present with myself and present with Daniel, rather than stuck in my own inner agony of resistance.

CHALLENGES CREATE DEEP ROOTS

My aunt used to say, "That which doesn't kill you makes you stronger." I'm reminded of the unexpected lesson of Biosphere 2, a closed-system habitat experiment conducted in the 1990s. Built in the desert of southern Arizona (and now owned by the University of Arizona), the domed structure was a research tool for scientists to study Earth's living systems by creating a contained miniature version of our planet.

To the dismay of the scientists, trees in the biosphere were collapsing before reaching maturity. The scientists noticed that the trees' wood was soft and their roots were shallow. Obviously, a tree needs a strong trunk and deep roots in order to flourish.

The trees' poor health baffled scientists until they linked it to the one missing element in the biosphere: wind. It turns out that wind stress is necessary for the healthy growth of a tree—resistance to the wind causes the tree to grow stronger.

Just as environmental stress is required for a tree to grow sturdy, so, perhaps, it is with us humans. When you face your next challenging circumstance, see it as the wind you need in order to grow stable and resilient. When you view your circumstances as potentially helpful, it becomes easier to align with them.

66 *Wind stress is necessary for the healthy growth of a tree—resistance to the wind causes the tree to grow stronger.* **99**

BLESSING OR CURSE?

Is a situation a challenge or a "blessing in disguise"? Sometimes it's hard to be sure. I try to remember this when I listen to the news, a litany of one tragedy after another. I remind myself that, in a world of heart-wrenching situations, there are always moments of grace and beauty as well.

Often, there is a fine line between good and bad fortune. The rain that the bride curses is the same rain that the farmer blesses. A famous Buddhist parable illustrates this conundrum:

Once upon a time there was an old farmer. One day his mule ran away. Upon hearing the news, his neighbors came over. "Such bad luck", they said sympathetically. "Maybe", the farmer replied.

The next morning the mule returned, bringing with it three wild horses. "How wonderful", the neighbors exclaimed. "Maybe", replied the old man.

The following day, his son tried to ride one of the untamed horses, was thrown and broke his leg. The neighbors came again. "What misfortune", they lamented. "Maybe", answered the farmer.

The day after, officials came to the village to draft young men into the army. Seeing that the son's leg was broken, they passed him by. The neighbors congratulated the farmer on how well things had turned out. "Maybe", said the farmer.

> **"** *The circumstances that may seem initially the hardest to accept could turn out to be the very circumstances that benefit us the most.* **"**

The farmer understands that you cannot really know how an event will play out. Any single event causes a multitude of consequences that often are not clear until the future arrives. Circumstances are constantly arising, changing and unfolding into new circumstances.

Who's to know what circumstances will end up being positive and which will end up being negative? The world is not always as it seems. In terms of helping us grow or inspiring us to be our best selves, the circumstances that may seem initially the hardest to accept could turn out to be the very circumstances that benefit us the most. Letting go of our story about the future allows us to neutralize our circumstances and ultimately accept them as they are.

IMPERMANENCE

Meanwhile, there is no doubt that favorable circumstances are preferred. There is nothing like a charmed day on which you are healthy and rested, on which you feel abundant and in love with life itself, on which you notice beauty everywhere. On days like this, everything is "just right".

Unfortunately, if you need your circumstances to be "just right" in order to be happy, then woe betide you. Circumstances are like a moving river, always changing and always shifting. You can't get them to freeze. Just when everything is perfect, something changes. Then everything feels imperfect all over again.

Everything is in flux—feelings change, circumstances change. This realization of impermanence helps us savor and enjoy the good aspects of life while they last. It helps us tolerate and accept what seems bad because we remember that it's not forever.

❝ *Circumstances are like a moving river, always changing and always shifting.* **❞**

In another ancient parable, there was a king who sought a phrase that could be his shining light, his guide through good times and bad. He called upon all the wise people in the land, asking them for the perfect words that would be a compass for every circumstance. One of the wise men brought him a ring inscribed with the phrase "This Too Shall Pass". The king kept the ring. When things were going well, he read the phrase and it kept him humble. When things were going poorly, he also read the phrase, and it kept his heart from being too heavy.

Whether you can see your circumstances as beneficial or not, whether you can change your circumstances or not, whether they are easy to accept or difficult, **always remember that impermanence is a quality of all things**. Let this knowledge aid you in the passage from resistance to alignment to possibility.

KICK IT UP A NOTCH

As we know, how you accept your circumstances can vary in intensity. To advance the journey from "allow without protest" to "enthusiastic embrace", experiment with a willingness to see every circumstance as occurring for your *benefit*. You may not know why or understand any of it, but what would happen if you thought every single event was the best thing that could be happening to you?

When I went on a trip to India in 2007 with my best friend, I had just read a very powerful and intriguing little book by Chris Prentiss called *Zen and the Art of Happiness*. The following phrase really caught my attention: "Every event that befalls me is absolutely the best possible event that could occur."

My friend and I decided to make that phrase our trip motto and we used it many times each day. In fact, we had a hilarious time using it when our flight was delayed, when we got lost in Old Delhi, when we were served unidentifiable food, when we were standing on crowded train platforms— even when one of us had our wallet stolen. Those were the challenges that we tried to meet with curiosity and welcome.

> **❝** *Every event that befalls me is absolutely the best possible event that could occur.* **❞**

As a result, we had an amazing trip. Every day was an adventure, full of color and scent and magic and mystery. Nothing became a problem and every situation was wrapped in the mystery of "Hmmmm, I don't really see how this could be for my benefit, but I know it is, so I am willing to hold out that possibility!" Our resistance to our circumstances faded and our self-fulfilling prophecy of benefit became manifest.

Try it for a day and see if it doesn't revolutionize the way you see your world unfolding. How would your experience of life change if you really believed that everything was happening for your benefit?

POWER TOOLS

PRIMARY TOOL: GO WITH THE FLOW

The next time you wash your hands, feel the water flowing out of the tap. Sense the texture, the temperature and pressure, the flow of the water as it cascades over your fingers. Take an intentional pause, breathe deeply, and accept this singular moment. Say to yourself, "This is now. All I have is today, this moment. I am here, now. I go with the flow. I choose to flow with life rather than against it. I accept this moment and I let it be just as it is."

BONUS TOOL: WRITING EXERCISE

Write a letter to a dear friend or family member, pretending that they have the exact same set of circumstances that you are currently struggling with. For example, if you were battling health problems, you would write to your friend as if she had just been given that diagnosis. What might you say to her? Share your empathy and your concern, your advice and wisdom. Let her know how you can offer her support. Open your heart and be with her as she faces her challenge. What can you write to help her reframe her situation?

Optional extra: One week later, mail this letter to yourself. When you receive the letter, read it as though you are the friend, receiving this advice and love and empathy from yourself. How does it feel to receive this kind of friendship and support from you after time has passed?

BONUS TOOL: PAUSE. BREATHE. SMILE.

Mother Teresa said that "peace begins with a smile". Try it: Pause. Breathe. Smile. Smiling is known to affect moods positively. The act of smiling activates neural messaging by stimulating the release of the "feel-good" neurotransmitters (dopamine, serotonin, and endorphins) and also compounds called neuropeptides, all of which have many major benefits to the body, brain and moods.

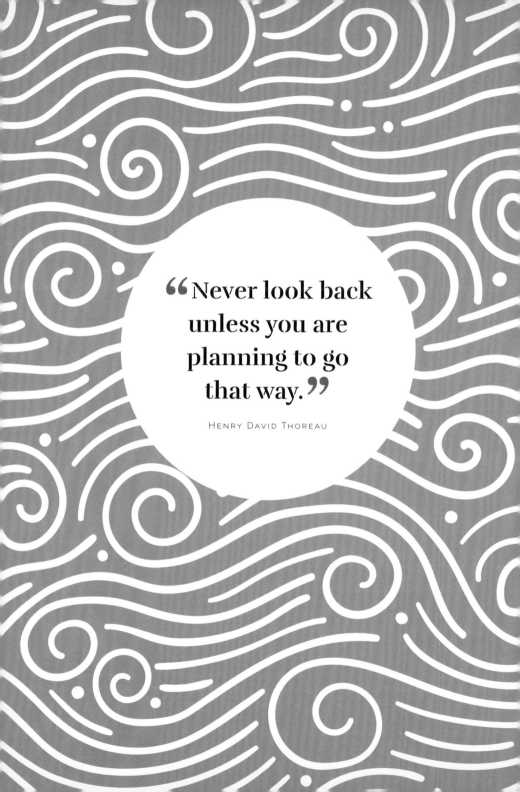

"Never look back unless you are planning to go that way."

HENRY DAVID THOREAU

6

ACCEPTING THE PAST

Once again, Roger reached for a tissue, his eyes brimming with tears. Every week for the past two months, Roger had come into the session berating himself, ruminating about how things might have been different... if only. Roger was a bereaved father and he felt a heavy weight of responsibility for his son's death.

Although Roger wasn't actually responsible for his son's death, he couldn't help believing that things would have gone differently if he had made different decisions. Sometimes the pain of taking responsibility is easier to endure than realizing that, in truth, you had absolutely no control.

For five years, Roger had ridden the wild rollercoaster of his son's heroin addiction. CJ had been a troubled young man. He had struggled with a learning disability in school, had suffered from depression throughout his young adulthood and had found solace in a drug that ruled his life. Roger had supported CJ through detox visits, rehabs, and 12-Step programs (see page 28).

But the night before CJ overdosed, presumably by accident, Roger had kicked him out of the family home. Roger had taken the route of tough love, telling CJ that Dad was no longer going to be an enabler and that CJ wasn't welcome until he could get clean and sober. The next day, CJ was found unconscious in a friend's apartment. Roger, overcome with grief, had sat beside him while he was on life support for five days. Roger begged, pleaded, prayed and willed him to get better, but it was not to be. The doctors told Roger that CJ was braindead and so, on the eve of CJ's 29th birthday, Roger made the decision to pull the plug.

> **66** *The problem with regret
> is that you can never, and I
> mean never, undo the past.* **99**

"If only I hadn't sent him away that night..." Roger cried out for the hundredth time. If only. If only. If only.

There was no consolation for Roger. It didn't help for him to think that if it hadn't been that night, it might have been another night. After all, CJ had been on a self-destructive course for years. It also didn't help for Roger to understand that his decision that night had made sense, given everything he knew and had done up to that point.

These logical explanations weren't helpful. The problem with regret is that you can never, and I mean *never*, undo the past. What's done is done. Yet, we play incessant head games with ourselves by ruminating over and over again on circumstances that have already occurred, as if they might play out differently if we play the tape in our minds one more time. We desperately dream that we can change the outcome.

While Roger knew, on some level, that his regret and guilt were unproductive emotions, and while he longed for a sense of peace, he just couldn't see his way out. But his pain was overwhelming and, in the end, it was his longing for relief that opened his heart to the ACT practice (see Chapter 2). In fact, the "A" (**Acknowledge**) of ACT came easily to him. He could say to himself, "Roger, I know you're in so much pain. I see that you feel responsible. I know you wish things could have gone differently. This is horrible." The simple act of acknowledging his own suffering brought tears of release.

From this place of awareness, Roger also had a relatively easy time with the "C" (**Connect**) of ACT. He could easily connect with the struggle of the many parents he had met in treatment centers and Alanon meetings (for family and friends of alcoholics). He had felt a bond with the bereaved parents in "The Compassionate Friends" meetings (for bereaved family members). He said to himself, "Roger, you are among thousands of people who love and have loved an addict. You are in the good company of so many bereaved parents who have done their best and still have broken hearts."

But when it came time to **Talking kindly** to himself—the "T" of ACT— this was much more of a challenge for Roger. At first, he simply couldn't muster a way to do so. "I just want to beat myself up," he said. So we stayed with that, admitting how hard it was to be gentle with himself, acknowledging how much of a challenge it was to even think of cutting himself some slack.

Sometimes if clients are having trouble accessing any gentle words for themselves, I invite them to shift their focus to the body. Attending to emotional sensations as felt in the body is the entrance to a softening. We both closed our eyes and I asked Roger if he could describe how it felt in his body to feel like he just wanted to beat himself up.

"It feels tight in my chest. Actually wait, no—more like clenched in my stomach, like I've been kicked in the gut," he reported.

"Okay, right, kicked in the gut", I repeated. "Can you just let that be there, just notice it, watch it. Notice what happens when you just sit with that feeling, that sensation in your gut."

"I don't like it", he responded. "I want to *not* be with it."

"Yes, it's uncomfortable", I replied. "But notice what it's like to stay with it, if you can, to be present with it a bit longer, allowing it to simply be there, to express its pain. I invite you to say to yourself that you just wanted to be a good father and you wanted to help CJ but couldn't."

Roger teared up as I said it. "That's it. I just wanted to help him but I was helpless."

"It's okay to honor that feeling, Roger. Where do you notice the helplessness in your body?" I prompted.

"I just want to collapse like a rag doll. Like there's no stuffing in me. I have no power. I don't like this."

"Yes, no one would want that feeling of having no power, of having no stuffing", I soothed. "Watch as your body lets this be—this feeling of powerlessness. Let that feeling, that sensation, just be there. Even the feeling of not liking it, that's all right, too."

We were silent for a while and Roger spontaneously put his hand on his stomach. "I just want to feel better", he said. "Right now, I feel bad and, at the same time, somehow not as bad."

"See if you can just stay with this a bit longer", I encouraged. "What's happening in your body now?"

"Well, the tightness in my chest is gone. I feel a little more relaxed, actually", he said. "And I have this sense of something, some feeling toward my powerlessness, not pity but...well, tenderness maybe? Like it's horrible when you can't be all-powerful but I'm just human. I'm just a man who loved my son."

Roger made the shift, right there. He was able to move into a softer place toward himself because he acknowledged his suffering, he allowed it to be. He activated his witnessing self by describing his own experience. In so doing, he accepted his resistance to the suffering and created space for a shift in perspective. After this session, he was able to talk kindly to himself on his own, to remind himself that he was only human. His moments of suffering became moments of self-compassion and comfort.

For Roger, the word "acceptance" never felt right, but he could tolerate the word "allow". He chose to "allow" his past to be as it was, nothing more, nothing less. His self-talk shifted to words of gentle encouragement to move forward, to honor CJ's memory and carry on, unburdened by guilt. Upon allowing CJ's death to be part of his life, Roger looked ahead (to possibility) and realized that he didn't want to waste the time left to him. He chose to start embracing life again, in honor of CJ.

* Accepting your past does *not* mean that you liked it or you wish to relive it.

* Accepting your past *does* mean that you move on, using the past for growth.

SELF-FORGIVENESS

To forgive yourself is to stop feeling angry or resentful toward yourself. Self-forgiveness and self-acceptance feel very much the same. Each is an act of relaxing into the reality of what you've got, each a letting go of resistance, each a shift to a gentler relationship with yourself. Accepting that you did something that you wish you hadn't—or even accepting that you didn't do some things that you wish you had—is a kind of self-forgiveness. Maybe you made a mistake. Perhaps you would have done something differently based on the results. Possibly you did something really hurtful. Or maybe you even committed a crime.

Remember Claude Anshin Thomas, the Vietnam veteran turned Zen Buddhist monk (see page 82)? The people at Plum Village kept telling him that "the past is in the past". He finally exploded and exclaimed, "The past is not always in the past—sometimes it's in the present moment and it's not beautiful and I hate it." He was haunted by the fact that he had murdered innocent people in the war. One of the monks said to him, "One just needs to learn how to live with this experience like still water."

It took Claude three years to forgive himself, but he finally started to live quietly alongside the memories of his own past behavior. For Claude, as he let go of his anger and resentment toward himself, acceptance and forgiveness merged into one. Part of the art of accepting the past when you are "to blame" is embracing self-forgiveness, and **for some it might also include an act of atonement.**

“ *To forgive yourself is to stop feeling angry or resentful toward yourself.* **”**

MAKING AMENDS

Addiction programs based on the 12 Steps have a practice of taking an inventory of a person's shortcomings and making amends where appropriate. Religious traditions also support the idea of confession and atonement. When we commit a wrongdoing, the acts of confessing, atoning, apologizing and making amends are ways to demonstrate our acceptance of the past and pave the path for self-forgiveness.

Carlos was desperate to turn his life around. When he came to see me, he was 42 years old and suffering from depression. His father had recently passed away, plunging Carlos into an emotional tailspin. "We were never very close, really. I resented that he was an alcoholic when I was growing up. He wasn't the kind of dad who went to my baseball games, if you know what I mean."

Carlos had thought that if he ignored his dad, shutting him out of his life, he could be rid of his influence. But Carlos had been blaming his father for his entire life: "I realized that bastard gave me only one thing—a bitter perspective on life."

When Carlos's father was sick and dying the previous year, Carlos hadn't gone to visit him. He had considered it but then decided, "That man was never there for me when he was alive, so why I should I be there for him when he's dying?"

When Carlos started working with me, he kept blaming his father for his own depression. Our work revolved around helping Carlos to be gentle with himself in ways that his father was never able to be. With self-compassion came Carlos's realization that his happiness was his responsibility and within his own control. He struggled with his guilt for not having visited his dad on his deathbed. He regretted his decision, and the image of his father dying all alone pulled incessantly on his heart strings.

It was the power of this image that eventually influenced Carlos to become a hospice volunteer. Self-compassion had, for Carlos, enlivened his awareness of compassion for others, even for his father. He told me that he could be available to other dying people even though he hadn't been there for his own dying father. "I'm kind of doing this for my dad, in his honor. He was a bastard but he wasn't all bad, you know?" For Carlos, volunteering was a way of making amends. With this full acceptance of his past behavior, he was able to move forward in his own life without berating himself for deeds undone. He was able to derive new meaning from his past and transcend his suffering.

IN THE PAST OR IN THE PRESENT?

But what if you weren't the one to blame, the one who fell short? What if someone else is responsible for your difficult past? How do you accept and move on? Do you forgive or forget? Part of the art of accepting the past when you are not responsible is to acknowledge that past as simply part of who you are now, perhaps even as the fuel that moved you to your current stronger self.

That's how it was for Laura who came to see me after a small car accident. This experience had left her with anxiety and an overwhelming fear of approaching intersections (she had been rear-ended while at a stop sign). As it turned out, she was also very unhappy in her life. She hated herself, hated her work and, since the car accident, frequently believed that she would be better off dead.

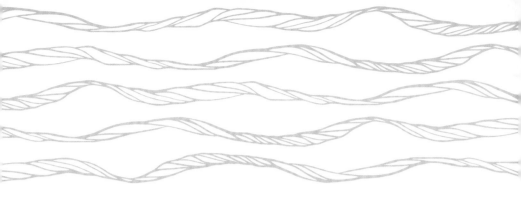

EMPLOYING RAPID EYE MOVEMENTS

Laura and I started our work together with a trauma technique called EMDR (Eye Movement Desensitization Reprocessing). This specific technique uses blinking lights which, when watched, move the eyes rapidly from side to side. As in REM (Rapid Eye Movement) sleep, the act of moving the eyes causes the brain to process memory. It also allows the brain to make memory associations and heal painful emotions.

When people engage in the trancelike process of moving their eyes right and left, right and left, their brain goes down a memory trail of associations. With Laura though we started with her memory of her car accident, the process of EMDR took her mind elsewhere.

I stopped the light sensors and asked her, "What do you notice?" (She had been instructed to report any images or feelings arising.) She said, "Well, I just had an image of being in my room when I was a kid, and I was playing with my dolls when my dad just burst into my room, yelling at me. He came over and smacked me on the head. Wow, I haven't thought of that in years." Her father had been an alcoholic with a violent temper when he was drunk.

We kept the EMDR processing going and, as Laura's brain healed itself, one image after another of her father's abusive behavior arose and receded from her mind. She began to cry but continued to follow the lights and report the images that she saw. She remembered multiple times when he did what she called "smack attacks", when he would burst into her room drunk and beat her for no apparent reason.

Sniffling, she said, "I remember so many times when he told me that he wished I was a boy and that I never should have been born."

Laura was so brave as she let these memories surface and integrate with her adult self. She hadn't thought about these painful incidents in years. Suddenly, she looked up, realizing why the car accident—a shocking attack from behind—had triggered her anxiety. And she realized why it had also triggered that feeling that she'd be better off dead, just as she had felt when she was growing up. At the end of this session, freed from her trauma, her feeling of distress had dissipated and she felt a new-found calm.

When we began to unpack her painful and abusive childhood, she came to realize that the residual effects of her past had played out in her present life. In fact, most people don't realize how much past experiences, especially from childhood, often bear upon the present day. **To the unconscious, there is no linear time...the past actually is the present.**

MAKING PEACE WITH THE PAST

With the trauma healed, Laura wanted to fortify her self-esteem, her inner sense of value and competence. She needed to sever her identification with her childhood belief that she was somehow flawed or deserving of abuse. She was ready for self-compassion.

Laura and I embarked on a series of guided visualizations in which her present-day self sat with her child self. Laura was able to see herself holding, soothing, and comforting her little-girl self, telling her that she was not alone and that she didn't deserve the treatment she had received.

Laura is fortunate because it was fairly easy for her to forgive her father. He had been beaten by his own father, so she saw him as an injured person himself. Self-compassion was the starting point for Laura, for accepting her father for who he was and for accepting her own past. She knew that her current adult strength was a direct result of being a survivor. She came to see her childhood as a piece in the puzzle of her life, but only a small piece.

"I think of my past as compost," she said. "It's just garbage but you let it ripen and it turns into this fertile, life-giving organic matter."

Laura welcomed the feeling that she was a valuable and worthwhile person and was able to integrate that feeling into her current sense of self. Today, she is a strong and vibrant woman: a survivor.

If we look back on our acceptance journey, we see that often our very difficulties are also our best teachers: difficulties with ourselves, with others, with circumstances and, yes, even with all of those curious and distressing events from the past.

SPACIOUSNESS AND PERSPECTIVE

Sometimes you simply need a little distance, some perspective, to see it all with a bit more clarity. Consider this story from the Hindu tradition:

A Hindu master grew tired of his apprentice complaining and so, one morning, sent him for some salt. When the apprentice returned, the master instructed the unhappy young man to put a handful of salt in a glass of water and then to drink it.

"How does it taste?" the master asked.

"Bitter," spluttered the apprentice.

The two walked in silence to a nearby lake. The master asked the young man to mix a handful of salt in the lake. When the apprentice had finished stirring salt into the water, the old man said, "Now drink from the lake."

The young man did so and then the master asked, "How does it taste?"

"Fresh," noted the apprentice.

"Do you taste the salt?" asked the master.

"No," said the young man.

At this, the master took the hands of the serious young man and offered this reflection: "The pain of life is pure salt; no more, no less. The amount of pain in life remains the same, exactly the same. But the bitterness we taste depends on the container we put the pain in. So, when you are in pain, the only thing you can do is to enlarge your awareness. Stop being a glass. Become a lake."

Self-compassion enlarges our spaciousness for acceptance. Acceptance enlarges our spaciousness for possibility. When we truly notice the past as the past, a wide vista opens before us. What felt unacceptable, what was once too bitter to tolerate, is now simply a small piece of a spacious personal history. The past is over. The present is now. The future is yet to be.

PAST/PRESENT/FUTURE

Just as the past affects our present, our present affects our future. Everything we do and think today is going to be our past tomorrow. All we have to work with is today, this moment, right now.

I once had a 32-year-old client, Rebecca, who had begun smoking more than ten years before. She berated herself for being a smoker, for having poisoned her body for a decade. She was fixated on the past and why she had even started smoking in the first place. The strength of her resistance against her past choices and against her current cravings was evident in her clenched body and her negative self-talk.

Over several sessions, I guided Rebecca down the path of self-compassion and she became kinder to herself. That didn't mean that she changed her behavior right away, but it did mean that she freed herself from self-loathing, from the resistance that had paralyzed her ability to change. She didn't like her past choices or her current cravings,

> **“** *Just as the past affects our present, our present affects our future.* **”**

but she was coming to terms with them. And what I noticed was that, as she moved into a sort of neutral acceptance ("the past is over"), her kind self-talk evolved into an inner cheerleader. ("Rebecca, it's hard to quit, but you can do this. You are not alone in making this change. You deserve the healthy choice.") With no resistance to her past, she was able to create a new day, a day that her future self could look back on with gratitude.

"I guess I can't drive forward if I keep staring into the rear-view mirror", Rebecca said suddenly at the end of the session. For her, moving into the future was ultimately about not looking backward any more.

Self-compassion helped Rebecca to move from alignment ("I was a smoker for years and am even a smoker right now") to possibility ("Something different is possible and I'm open to it"). While she couldn't change her behavior of the past, she could believe in the possibility of changing her behavior today.

KICK IT UP A NOTCH

If you want to take accepting the past from mild "allowing without protest" to "enthusiastic embrace", you can intensify your experience by thinking even more spaciously about the concept of karma—and, if you are so inclined, all the way back to possible past lives.

At its most basic, the Buddhist and Hindu idea of karma refers to the causes and effects of behavior. The negative or positive actions we take in one moment will have some residual effect on our future moments. When taken with a belief in reincarnation, the idea is that what we experience in this lifetime is directly related to experiences from previous lifetimes. Furthermore, your soul may have agreed to the circumstances of this life as necessary for its ongoing growth!

> **❝Be open to exploration... and mystery...and acceptance.❞**

Karma and rebirth may or may not be comfortable views for you. But, even if they feel foreign, you may still gain some inspiration from musing upon the perspective they offer. How could your current circumstances have been impacted by your previous behavior? How could your present behavior affect your future self? Why might your soul have wanted your current situation for personal growth? Even if you don't have the answers, invite the questions. Be open to exploration...and mystery... and acceptance.

POWER TOOLS

PRIMARY TOOL: SENSORY GROUNDING

Surrendering the past is ultimately about being in the present. Wake up to this moment, right now. Select an object to hold, to assist in your five-senses awakening exercise.

See: Notice the details of the object as you hold it. Pause and really see the nuances, the colors, the light reflected from it. Notice whether the details sharpen or get fuzzy as you bring it into your awareness.

Touch: Feel the details of this object as you hold it. Is the texture rough or smooth? Cold or warm? Soft or hard? Experience the sensations and notice if they feel different on your fingertips than on your palm.

Hear: Shake your object. Does it make a noise? Does it make a sound when you bring it up to your ear? What about the sound of your fingers on the object? Experience or imagine the noise it might make when banged or rubbed against other surfaces.

Taste: If this is an object to taste, do so. If not, then notice the taste in your mouth as your other senses take in your object.

Smell: Does your object have a fragrance? If not, what aromas are in this space with you? Imagine them circling and infusing your object.

Practice being in this moment and only this moment.

BONUS TOOL: CONNECTION STRETCH

Standing or sitting, prepare to visualize your life's timeline, linking the past, present and future, as you stretch into it.

1 Bend over and drop your hands to the earth—this is your past.

2 Reach your hands high up to the sky—this is your future.

3 Come back to the center, with your hands in a Namaste position (a yoga position in which hands are pressed together, fingers pointing upward, and thumbs close to the chest)—this is the present moment.

4 Inhale deeply and exhale knowing that you are moving into the future and creating a new past moment, even as you are living in the now.

BONUS TOOL: BITTERSWEET MEMORIES

Take a few minutes to identify a difficult experience from the past (something bitter) and see if you can come up with two aspects of it that were not so bad (something sweet).

For example, I remember seventh grade at school being a very unhappy year—my parents divorced that year and I was squarely in the awkward phase. But what I remember fondly about that same time is:

✳ absolutely loving my piano teacher and how kind she was to me, bringing chocolate chip cookies to my lessons since she knew I was going through a hard time;

✳ winning the junior high school spelling bee, which was a big award and quite exciting for a 13-year-old.

Another example: I remember, when all three of my children were quite young, I had an emergency appendectomy. This was scary, inconvenient, and painful. But I also remember fondly:

✳ my best friend and neighbor coming to help babysit my children, bringing me homemade soup and even washing my laundry;

✳ one nurse in particular who was an absolute angel, as she took incredible care of me in the hospital and helped me manage the pain.

When you look for sweet memories, you will find them...even in the midst of the bitter ones.

66 *When you look for sweet memories, you will find them...even in the midst of the bitter ones.* 99

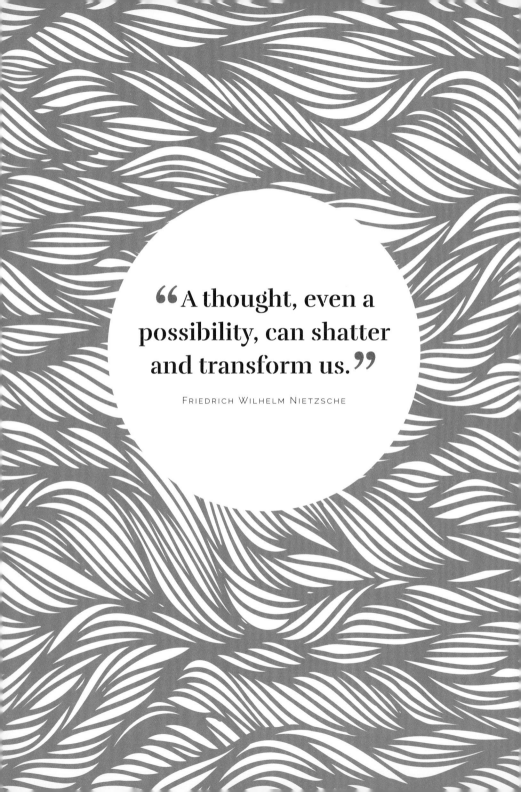

"A thought, even a possibility, can shatter and transform us."

FRIEDRICH WILHELM NIETZSCHE

7

LIVING WITH POSSIBILITY

A man arrives home to find that a huge pile of manure has been dumped in front of his house. He didn't order it. He does not want it. He is annoyed by it. But somehow, it's there. As we learned in Chapter 1, his response may correspond to various stages in the acceptance process. He can complain about it, ranting and raving about his rotten luck in life **(resistance)**. He can leave it there and without resistance simply allow this new circumstance to be **(alignment)**. Even better, upon aligning with it, he can calmly reflect on what might happen next—he could sell it or spread it around his garden as fertilizer **(possibility)**.

We all face the same choice when dealing with life and its various challenges. We can resist or accept. We don't ask for challenges; we don't want them. Yet, in the end, how we respond to them sets the stage for our future, for possibility.

Living with possibility means being curious and open to the future, and saying to yourself, "This is what I've got—now what's next?" We may or may not have control over specific details, but we do have control over our attitude of acceptance.

* Acceptance does *not* mean that there's no hope for change.

* Acceptance *does* mean that you are at the doorway of possibility.

BAD OR BETTER?

Gracie was 32 years old, happily pregnant, and terrified of all things medical. When she came to see me, she wanted to work on her fear of childbirth—including her fear of needles, intravenous drips, and having blood taken, not to mention her terror of actually giving birth. Her resistance was palpable. She had considered a home birth to avoid medical environments, but her husband wasn't comfortable with that option. So she was preparing for the inevitable...with both fists clenched.

Together we practised the ACT process (see Chapter 2) around her feelings of fear and anxiety. As with all acceptance, self-compassion is the first step. Gracie acknowledged and felt what it was like to accept her anxiety, "Gracie, you're worried and your worry makes sense. This is a big deal and your body is such a precious vessel."

As we continued the ACT practice, I asked Gracie to close her eyes and visualize herself lying in a hospital bed, with a nurse nearby whose job was to help her. "Now imagine this nurse preparing to take your blood. She is tying a band around your arm and looking at your veins to determine where to begin."

Across from me, Gracie's entire body visibly tensed. It was as if resistance were literally coursing through her veins as she readied herself for assault.

"What's happening in your body right now?" I asked.

"I'm tightening, bracing for it," she said.

"Okay, now see if you can focus on your breath. Pause in your tightening and breathe. Drop your attention to your center. Breathe deeply." I continued to guide her: "Gracie, this is scary but you're not alone. Lots of people are nervous in medical situations. You will make it through this as you have at other times. Notice your options. Do you resist it and increase your pain or do you align with it and just go with the miracle of the modern needle? Tense up or go with the flow? It's your choice. What do you want?"

"I want it to be better, less miserable", she replied.

"Okay, you have the power to accept and move forward without resistance." I prompted, "Say to yourself, 'Breathe honey. You're going to be okay. You can trust that everyone here is doing their best to help you. You have the power to make this bad or better.'"

Gracie's body relaxed. She said to herself, "Yes, I can do this. I'm ready. I can make bad worse or bad better. That's how much power I have." And she exhaled long and low.

About two weeks later, I received an email from Gracie with a photo of the new baby. The birth had been a success. Not only had she had blood taken and an intravenous drip, but she had had an emergency Caesarean section. The new mother wrote, "I accepted what was happening and I knew I had a choice about how to go with it." And now she has a beautiful baby boy for all her efforts.

FROM CHRONIC RESISTANCE TO
A NEW WAY OF LIFE

Bruce is a 52-year-old man who, when we had our final session together, was full of gratitude. He wasn't simply grateful that he was feeling grounded, peaceful and happy (which hadn't been the case when we started our work together), but he was also feeling grateful that he was an alcoholic. Accepting that he was an alcoholic with the enthusiasm of a full body hug had changed the course of his life.

Bruce had initially come to see me after his wife had left him, at the end of her tether from his many nights of passing out drunk. In fact, he had been a heavy drinker for most of his adult life. He knew that it was too late to save his marriage but hoped that it was not too late to save himself. He told me, "I have a problem with alcohol and I can't seem to stop."

Bruce had already made a major leap. He had moved out of resistance and into alignment by admitting that, yes, he had a problem with alcohol. The ACT self-compassion practice was easy for Bruce. He experienced a feeling of surrender to his sadness, loss, and cravings.

"But what now?" he asked. What was he going to do with it? He could simply say, "Yep, I'm an alcoholic" and keep drinking—after all, he had accepted that he was a drinker. Or maybe there was another possibility.

The purpose of self-compassion is not to coddle yourself or give yourself permission for self-destructive behavior. Self-compassion is not meant to be a licence to do whatever you want, whenever you want. You might be compassionate to the child who doesn't want to wear a coat in freezing weather, but you would still insist that they wear the coat.

For Bruce, the ACT practice helped him move into possibility. He noticed his suffering. ("This is really hard, you basically keep drinking too much even when you think you can stop, and now you've lost your marriage.") He connected to a shared common experience. ("You're not the first person to have trouble with alcohol.") And his kind self-talk inspired him to shift. ("Okay, Bruce, you're an alcoholic. Yes, it's hard. But what do you want to do about it? You can turn this around and you don't have to do it by yourself. You can ask for help.") Sometimes talking kindly to yourself can feel like having a supportive coach, someone on your side who wants to encourage you.

Once Bruce accepted that he didn't need to tackle this alone, he opened up to the possibility of attending his first Alcoholics Anonymous meeting. He couldn't change that he was an alcoholic, but he could change his response to his condition. His inner journey expanded to an outer journey and the circumstances of his life started to change. Within a few weeks, he was sober and actively following the program of recovery. Bruce's happy ending began with accepting himself and aligning with his circumstances. With possibility came the knowledge that he had a choice about how to move forward.

Remember, when you cannot change your circumstances, acceptance opens up a world of other possibilities. When a door closes, look for a window.

"Self-compassion is not meant to be a licence to do whatever you want, whenever you want."

TRANSCENDING LOSS

When, in the 1990s, I wrote my first book, *Transcending Loss* (which I initially wanted to call "Look for the Window"), I was essentially interested in why some people were resilient after a major loss and able to grow, to make meaning and even to thrive, while other people became bitter and depressed. What I found was that transcendence, like acceptance, is a choice. As a griever comes to accept their painful feelings, love has room to thrive, and with it comes hope. Transcendence is a choice, to make meaning out of loss even while still heartbroken.

Also in the 1990s, the psychologists Richard G. Tedeschi and Lawrence G. Calhoun developed the concept of "post-traumatic growth" to explain how people who endure psychological distress following adversity can also experience positive emotional and personal growth. They observed, as I had, that individuals who endure suffering often initiate positive and meaningful personal change.

Emily is a middle-aged woman whose son committed suicide after returning from a tour of duty in the Iraq War. He was a victim of post-traumatic stress disorder. Every day, Emily still goes through a process of **resistance** (waking up and thinking, "No, he can't be dead") to **alignment** ("Yes, sadly he is dead") to **possibility** ("How can I honor his memory today?").

She has been active in counseling other bereaved mothers through The Compassionate Friends, a bereaved parents' organization. She has also been active in American Gold Star Mothers, an organization of mothers who have lost sons and daughters in the US Armed Forces. And she is tirelessly active in promoting suicide awareness, especially for veterans.

Would she give up her causes in a heartbeat if her son could miraculously come back? Yes. But is she determined to honor her love and turn her pain into something positive? Yes.

ACCEPTANCE AS AN APPROACH TO CHANGE

When people ask me, "How can a person simply accept injustices, global warming, poverty, abusive relationships, war?" I reply that acceptance is the entry point, the portal, and precursor to change. We have to start with what we've got. As Martin Luther King, Jr, said, "Darkness cannot drive out darkness; only light can do that. Hate cannot drive out hate; only love can do that." So, too, resistance cannot drive out resistance; only acceptance can do that.

Resistance is a form of darkness in which hate and dread abound. It is contracted, constricted, fearful, powerless. Acceptance illuminates the dark places of resistance. It is not only a bright light shining on our past and present, but also a peaceful approach to change, and it guides us into a better future.

Of course, resistance is a natural part of life's journey. And as we've seen, when we have compassion for our resistant state, when we validate our experience and then "pause, breathe, smile", we create the space to shift into alignment, a place of expansion, creativity and peace. It's from that place that we are free to spread our wings and fly into the world of possibility. That is the power of acceptance.

66 *Resistance cannot
drive out resistance;
only acceptance can
do that.* **99**

SPIRAL JOURNEYS

Life's journey can often feel like going around in circles. Sometimes it feels as though we are back where we started. But as we age and have the opportunity to look back on our lives, we realize that what felt like repetition was actually spiral movement; each time around moving up in the direction of gradual change—or sometimes down in a negative tailspin.

We are all familiar with the basics of momentum. Something takes a lot of energy to get going, but then seems to move forward with ease. Whether spiralling upward or downward, our lives can feel like they are moving with their own energy.

What we often fail to realize, in the midst of our journey, is how much our attitude toward life contributes to its movement. For example, when I worked at a mental health clinic in New York City, a friend of mine was laid off. I went into her office and said, "Janet, I'm so sorry this happened to you. Maybe one day you'll look back and see that this was somehow for the best."

She chuckled, "I don't know if it happened for a reason, but I'm going to *make it* turn out for the best."

I was moved by her easy acceptance of her circumstances and her optimistic attitude. Her acceptance allowed her to create the momentum for positive change, an upward spiral of her life trajectory. She was determined to look for the opportunities and the benefits that would reveal themselves. Had she got stuck in the position that getting laid off was the absolute worst occurrence possible, she would have created the momentum for the very reality that she feared.

66...there is nothing either good or bad, but thinking makes it so.99

WILLIAM SHAKESPEARE

CELLS WITH ATTITUDE

In the film *What the Bleep Do We Know!?* Dr. Joe Dispenza describes one of the ways that we literally program our bodies. When a new cell is produced, it isn't always an exact clone of the old cell; rather, the cell contains receptors for whatever peptide it received to cause the split. If the cell is flooded by "negative" peptides—produced by depression, for example—the new cells will have more receptors for that depression-related peptide. Thus, new cells are created literally according to what you think and feel. If you feel depressed for an hour, you've created hosts of new cells that have more receptors calling for the peptides linked to depression. Your current attitude creates momentum toward your future.

What you think, believe and feel in this moment becomes more and more true with each succeeding moment. We can create a battle or we can create peace.

We encounter this idea of momentum again and again. It's not what happens to you, it's what you do with what happens to you. The health psychologist Kelly McGonigal explained in "The Upside of Stress", her 2013 talk at TEDGlobal, that her research shows that it's not stress itself that causes heart attacks, but how you conceptualize stress. If you believe that your stress is going to be bad for your heart—if, in other words, you resist your stress—it is likely to be hard on your heart. But if you see your stress as beneficial, that it gives you focus and energy and motivation, and you align with it positively, then your stress can actually strengthen your response to life's challenges.

What does the "power of positive thinking" have to do with acceptance and self-compassion and possibility? Well, once you have been compassionate with your suffering and your struggle, once you have opened your heart to your own resistance, once you create the conditions for a shift to align with "what is", positive thinking becomes your natural position; you are open to possibility.

Shift questions

Here are three questions to ponder that are designed to help you see things from a new perspective and thus create an active shift from resistance to alignment to possibility. Reflect on each question and see if any insights arise.

* What kind of person do I want to be with what's happening?

* How might this be happening *for* me rather than *to* me?

* What's the higher invitation for me? How am I being invited to grow or to respond?

POSSIBILITY AND GRATITUDE

The perspective of acceptance helps you focus on the good among the bad, the flowers among the weeds. When we are in alignment with our circumstances, we have the freedom to shine the flashlight of our attention on what we're grateful for, on what is working rather than exclusively on what isn't working.

Dale, a widow I once knew, used gratitude to help her with her sorrow. She wasn't grateful that her husband died unexpectedly, but she was grateful for the many years of love that they had shared together. She was grateful that he had been her husband and had touched her life in so many happy and loving ways.

A question I sometimes ask to help grievers shift into gratitude is, "If I could wave a magic wand and take away all of the pain of your grief, but it also meant that I would take away your memories of ever having known your loved one...would you want the deal?" Almost everyone says, "No". They would choose to keep the pain of loss in order to keep the treasured memories of joy and love.

Dale was not only grateful for her past, but was also grateful for the ways her life had unfolded in her grief. She had met and shared her experiences with other widows, and she had shared her "pain poetry" on mourning websites which had been touchingly received by other grievers. Three years after her husband's death, she felt more generous, more spiritual and more compassionate with herself and others than she had before her loss.

Gratitude is a powerful alchemist for transforming pain into positivity. When you combine it with acceptance, you are launched into possibility.

It's fine if gratitude currently feels like a bit of a stretch. Sometimes curiosity is the best we can muster toward a situation. Ask yourself, "I wonder how this is going to lead to something good?" Or, "If everything is as it should be, I'm curious to see what's going to come of this and how." Or, "I wonder what will emerge that I will be grateful for." Or, "Why did this happen for me, instead of to me?" There are lessons embedded in every situation—we just have to relax and look.

66 *Gratitude is a powerful alchemist for transforming pain into positivity.* **99**

KICK IT UP A NOTCH

No book on acceptance would be complete without some discussion of our shared human fate: death. Yes, we can resist death if we want, pretending it will never happen. We can accept its inevitability with a nod or a handshake and then forget about it. Or we can smile into the wind and embrace our fate. Death will come regardless. But to embrace our fate, to accept death, releases us from the inhibition of fear and allows us to use our mortality as inspiration for a more meaningful life. Full acceptance of our mortality allows for the greatest freedom of all.

Stephen Covey, in his bestseller *The 7 Habits of Highly Effective People*, coined the phrase, "Begin with the end in mind" as Habit 2. He suggested that when you begin a task or project, you should have a clear vision of your desired destination and then keep moving to that point.

In discussing Habit 2, Covey suggests imagining your own funeral and what people are saying about you there, to help you evaluate your life so far. Acceptance of death allows for the clearest of visions so, to paraphrase Covey, begin each day with your death in mind. Knowing that your days are limited makes each of those days matter. Wouldn't you prefer to say at the end, "I lived my life with gusto, valued my time and had a wonderful, rich, meaningful life"? Is it possible for you to really befriend death, to live alongside it as a catalyst for *carpe diem*, for love, for acceptance? Would doing so allow you to live life more fully?

66 *Full acceptance of our mortality allows for the greatest freedom of all.* **99**

WHAT WILL YOUR DEATH DAY BE LIKE?

I sat beside his bed—his deathbed. Ralph and I had only met twice; he knew that he was dying and he was happy to talk about it. As a hospice volunteer, I had originally assumed that all hospice patients wanted to talk about dying. But many didn't. They wanted to talk about the weather, about their families, about their lives, but not about their dying. In our society, death is such a taboo topic...even to those on the verge of dying.

Ralph was 84 years old and he had embraced his destiny. He believed that he would be welcomed into the kingdom of heaven by a chorus of singing angels. He said, "I don't mind that I'm dying, but I wish that I had faced my mortality when I was young."

"Really?" I prompted. "What do you mean?"

"I mean, I always knew that I would die. Obviously. But I never lived like I was going to die," he said.

"What would you have done differently?" I asked.

"I wouldn't have worried so much, that's for sure," he replied wistfully. "That was all a pointless waste of precious time."

I waited to see if he had other reflections.

"And I would have had more fun, I think. Played more and relaxed more. And probably forgiven people more. Everyone was just doing the best they could. But then again, so was I."

Life—the dash
on the tombstone
between our birth date
and our death date.
How are you filling
your dash?

Ralph had accepted his present circumstances. His words were a beautiful example of compassion for others and himself. Ralph reminded me to live fully while there's time. Accepting that you are going to die is one thing, but letting mortality inspire vitality brings the highest degree of freedom.

About a week later, I got the call from my coordinator that Ralph had passed away peacefully. I reflected on how he had shown me to live with acceptance and die gracefully, without bitterness or anger. I imagined him singing with the angels.

Even with all its inherent struggles, life is still a gift. And when you hold that gift against the backdrop of mortality, you realize that the time to open up to life's possibilities is right this minute.

A plaque in the
catacombs of a church in
Rome says in five languages,
"What you are now we used
to be; what we are now
you will be."

POWER TOOLS

PRIMARY TOOL: THE GLAD GAME

Gratitude takes acceptance to a higher level, so it's a good muscle to exercise. The beloved fictional character Pollyanna (in the 1913 novel of the same name by Eleanor Porter) always played the "glad game" as a way to focus on something positive when in the midst of something negative. We can all benefit from the glad game at just about any time.

Take a moment to stop and intentionally focus on five things that you are grateful for right now. To count, they must be in your field of experience or field of vision. So, as I write this…"I'm glad that I have electricity." "I'm glad that I have heat (it's freezing outside)." "I'm glad that my sweet dog is on the floor beside me and I can hear him snoring." "I'm glad that I am happily anticipating a dinner date with my husband planned for tonight." "I'm glad for my comfortable office chair with the absolutely perfect lumbar support as I sit in front of my computer typing." "I'm glad that my computer is working properly", and so on.

You can also do the inverse and focus on what you are glad that you do not have at this particular moment. For example, right now, "I'm glad that I'm not in the hospital". "I'm glad that my car doesn't have a flat tire." "I'm glad that I don't have toothache." "I'm glad that I'm not homeless." "I'm glad that I'm not outside shovelling snow."

When you focus on gladness (either directly or inversely) from a place of acceptance, you magnify and expand your sense of gratitude about your life, and possibility becomes crystal clear. As you speak each gladness, close your eyes briefly and breathe in each one. Really let the gratitude soak into your consciousness, letting it settle into your bones. Feel the gladness. Savour the gladness. Absorb the gladness. Rejoice in the gladness!

BONUS TOOL: FUTURE-SELF EXERCISE

Watch yourself struggling in the present moment. Now create an image of your future self (ten years hence) sitting across the room. What do you look like? How do you stand or sit? What might you be wearing? Let your future self observe you, your current struggling self. Ask your future self, "What do you think of me?" "What do you notice?" "What do I need to pay attention to in my life right now?" "What advice do you have for me?" Listen to what your future self might want to tell your current self. Breathe and wait for the response from within. What possibilities float between here and there?

BONUS TOOL: VISUALIZATION

Resting in an imagined happy, calm place helps you to access the stillness within for creativity, insight and possibility.

Close your eyes and think of a special place, either a real one or an imagined one, where you feel completely at ease, relaxed, and accepted for who you are. Maybe it is a room in your childhood home, your favorite vacation location, a tropical beach or a spot of moss in a summer forest. See if you notice any sounds, colors, textures, aromas, or other details around you. Breathe in the scent of the place. Smile as you relish being in this completely relaxing and happy place. Feel the enchantment of it washing over you. Let yourself be happy here. This place of deep contentment and acceptance is the birthplace of possibility.

EPILOGUE

"We cannot change anything until we accept it."

CARL JUNG

At the start of every session with a client, I lead us in a brief mindfulness meditation. We simultaneously close our eyes and I say, "Relaxing into this moment, notice your breath...breathing in...and breathing out...let your body rest into the now. You are here. Allow yourself to gently be with what is, as it is, in this singular moment in time." Then I ring a Tibetan singing bowl three times, saying "breathe in the bell", and we listen to the final ring as it slowly dissipates.

My clients have come to love the bell routine. Even my beagle, Copper, who graces my sessions with his presence, seems to "breathe in the bell"! This simple ritual serves a few different purposes. It invites a pause in the rush of a busy day. It joins our energies as my client and I formally begin our session together. And it gives me a chance to seed an implicit message of compassion and acceptance. Although I don't use either of those words in this meditation, I encourage those very concepts by inviting a gentle atmosphere of "welcome" into the room.

And as you well know after reading this book, self-compassion and acceptance are the building blocks of a happier, more peaceful experience with life itself. When you ride on the raft of nonjudgemental acceptance, you flow with the river of "what is".

Having spent the last year writing this book immersed in the practice of acceptance, I am more certain than ever of its power. As I allowed this work to impact my own life, I marinated in the acceptance journey, moving from resistance to alignment to possibility. I soaked myself in self-compassion and reflected on the process. I drenched myself in curiosity again and again, showered in the warmth of active acceptance.

Acceptance is the bridge that takes you
from suffering to awakening, the land of inner
peace and personal transformation.

JUST SAY YES

In the 2008 film *The Yes Man*, Jim Carrey plays a man who has been inspired by a guru to "just say yes"...to everything. He says yes to the homeless man who needs a lift. He says yes to his friends who want him to keep drinking. He says yes to the woman who offers him a ride on her motorcycle. This hilarious premise opens him to a host of adventures, including a new love and positive life changes.

While self-acceptance has always been a powerful go-to strategy for me, I wondered to myself what it would be like to accept everything. Could I walk the talk? What struggles might I encounter as I sought peace in the corners of my life that I currently resisted?

I took the challenge and said, "I accept" for delays, changes in scheduling and people cutting me off in traffic. I actively accepted my resistance when I heard that my father had been diagnosed with prostate cancer. I actively accepted myself on each part of the journey, always with the goal of alignment. Son not coming home for Christmas? I accept. Another snowstorm in February? I accept. Stomach flu? I accept. Stepdaughter having an emergency operation? I accept.

Sometimes my reactions toward life's challenges were charged with frustration, sadness, anger or fear. And I accepted those, too. To say "yes" to acceptance meant leaning into my pain with acknowledgement and with kindness. Oh my, does life have plentiful opportunities for practice!

All I can say is that, yes, living with acceptance at the forefront of my mind for an entire year, using acceptance as my guiding light, really did create a profound and noticeably positive shift in my life. It didn't always happen quickly or easily. Fortunately, self-compassion was my friendly companion, helping me to acknowledge my struggle, connecting to the world of others who shared my experience, and talking kindly to myself in the process. In the end, I was able to align with the journey, however difficult, and attend to myself, moment to moment.

What I noticed along the way was that micro-shifts in my resistance opened to deeper shifts. My heart opened degree by degree as I came into alignment with each circumstance. I was able to relax into what was happening without fighting it so much, and life flowed. Gifts unfolded where I hadn't seen them before.

Remember that when you allow the process of acceptance to unfold, it *does not* mean that you actually like what you are accepting. Nor does it mean that change is impossible. But it *does* mean that you relax into the moment without struggle. The moment you accept the pain, you lessen the suffering. When you truly let it be, with compassion, you then have the freedom to turn toward the future.

"Deep peace of the running wave to you.
Deep peace of the flowing air to you.
Deep peace of the quiet earth to you.
Deep peace of the shining stars to you."

GAELIC BLESSING

THE ART AND THE POWER

The **art** of acceptance is evident in the choices you make along the journey. How do you engage your own resistance? How compassionate are you with yourself? Are you able to align with ease? Does simply "allowing" feel right or do you long to lean in and kick it up a notch? How you navigate the process is based on your unique background, needs and personality.

The **power** of acceptance is experienced as inner peace and possibility. When you move from a closed door to an open one, a new world opens to you. In accepting yourself, accepting other people, accepting your circumstances and accepting your past, you become free...freer than you ever thought possible.

Self-compassion is the key to boosting and expanding the power of acceptance. Why? Because when you apply self-compassion to yourself, to your every feeling, your resistance fades and you find yourself in a very different relationship with your world. You naturally start to have more compassion for all beings. This puts you in a place of feeling deeply connected to all that is, exactly as it is. Some call this enlightenment, some identify it as awakening, and some say it is just pure acceptance.

Your time is now. Savour it. Live it. Love it. Accept it.

*" May your acceptance journey be
a portal to higher ground. "*

IN SUMMARY...

What acceptance is not:

1
Acceptance is not the same thing as apathy.

2
Acceptance does not mean giving up hope.

3
Acceptance is not a weakness.

4
Acceptance does not mean that whatever happened was alright or good.

5
Acceptance does not mean there cannot be change.

**What
acceptance
is:**

1
Acceptance is
about letting go
of resistance.

2
Acceptance
opens a portal
to more.

3
Acceptance
creates the energy
of flow.

4
Acceptance
is a pathway to
inner peace.

5
Acceptance
equals freedom.

REFERENCES AND FURTHER READING

Brach, Tara, *Radical Acceptance: Embracing Your Life with the Heart of a Buddha* (New York: Bantam, 2004).

Brown, Brené, *Daring Greatly: How the Courage to be Vulnerable Transforms the Way We Live, Love, Parent, and Lead* (New York: Avery, 2015).

Bush, Ashley Davis, *Hope and Healing for Transcending Loss: Daily Meditations for Those Who Are Grieving* (Newburyport, MA: Conari Press, 2016).

Bush, Ashley Davis, *Shortcuts to Inner Peace: 70 Simple Paths to Everyday Serenity* (New York: Berkley Books, 2011).

Bush, Ashley Davis, *The Little Book of Inner Peace: Simple Practices for Less Angst, More Calm* (London: Gaia, 2017).

Bush, Ashley Davis, *Transcending Loss: Understanding the Lifelong Impact of Grief and How to Make it Meaningful* (New York: Berkley Books, 1997).

Capretto, Lisa, "Eckhart Tolle Explains the Secret to Stress-free Living" (video of interview with Oprah Winfrey for *Super Soul Sunday*), *HuffPost*, https://www.huffingtonpost.com/2014/02/06/eckhart-tolle-stress_n_4732441.html, 2 June 2014, updated 6 June 2014 (accessed October 2018).

Covey, Stephen R, *The 7 Habits of Highly Effective People: Powerful Lessons in Personal Change* (New York: Simon & Schuster, 2013).

Davidson, Richard J and Sharon Begley, *The Emotional Life of Your Brain* (New York: Avery, 2012).

Desmond, Tim, *Self-compassion in Psychotherapy: Mindfulness-based Practices for Healing and Transformation* (New York: W W Norton, 2016).

Desmond, Tim, *The Self-compassion Skills Workbook: A 14-day Plan to Transform Your Relationship with Yourself* (New York: W W Norton, 2017).

Germer, Christopher K, *The Mindful Path to Self-compassion: Freeing Yourself from Destructive Thoughts and Emotions* (New York: The Guilford Press, 2009).

Gilbert, Paul, and Choden, *Mindful Compassion: How the Science of Compassion Can Help You Understand Your Emotions, Live in the Present, and Connect Deeply with Others* (Oakland, CA: New Harbinger Publications, 2014).

Graham, Linda, *Bouncing Back: Rewiring Your Brain for Maximum Resilience and Well-being* (Novato, CA: New World Library, 2013).

Hanson, Rick, *Resilient: How to Grow an Unshakable Core of Calm, Strength, and Happiness* (New York: Harmony Books, 2018).

Harris, Russ, *The Happiness Trap: How to Stop Struggling and Start Living: A Guide to ACT* (Durban, South Africa: Trumpeter Books, 2008).

Katie, Byron, *Loving What Is: Four Questions that Can Change Your Life* (New York: Three Rivers Press, 2003).

Korb, Alex, *The Upward Spiral: Using Neuroscience to Reverse the Course of Depression, One Small Change at a Time* (Oakland, CA: New Harbinger Publications, 2015).

Kornfield, Jack, *No Time Like the Present: Finding Freedom, Love, and Joy Right Where You Are* (New York: Atria Books, 2017).

Lesser, Elizabeth, *Broken Open: How Difficult Times Can Help Us Grow* (New York: Villard, 2005).

McGonigal, Kelly, *The Upside of Stress: Why Stress is Good for You, and How to Get Good at it* (New York: Avery, 2016).

Neff, Kristin, *Self-compassion: The Proven Power of Being Kind to Yourself* (New York: William Morrow, 2015).

Neff, Kristin, and Christopher Germer, *The Mindful Self-compassion Workbook: A Proven Way to Accept Yourself, Build Inner Strength, and Thrive* (New York: The Guilford Press, 2018).

Porter, Eleanor, *Pollyanna* (New York: Sterling Unabridged Classics, 2013).

Prentiss, Chris, *Zen and the Art of Happiness* (Malibu, CA: Power Press, 2006).

Schwartz, Richard C, *You are the One You've Been Waiting For: Bringing Courageous Love to Intimate Relationships* (Oak Park, IL: Center for Self Leadership, 2008).

Siegel, Dan, and Tina Payne Bryson, *The Yes Brain: How to Cultivate Courage, Curiosity, and Resilience in Your Child* (New York: Bantam, 2018).

Taylor, Shelley E, *The Tending Instinct: Women, Men, and the Biology of Nurturing* (New York: Holt Paperbacks, 2002).

Tedeschi, Richard G, and Bret A Moore, *The Posttraumatic Growth Workbook: Coming Through Trauma Wiser, Stronger, and More Resilient* (Oakland, CA: New Harbinger Publications, 2016).

Thomas, Claude Anshin, *At Hell's Gate: A Soldier's Journey from War to Peace* (Boston: Shambhala Press, 2006).

Tolle, Eckhart, *The Power of Now: A Guide to Spiritual Enlightenment* (Vancouver: Namaste Publishing, 2004).

Williamson, Marianne, *A Return to Love: Reflections on the Principles of "A Course in Miracles"* (New York: HarperOne, 1996).

INDEX

ACT (Acknowledge, Connect, Talk kindly) 53–62
alignment 36–40, 213–14
"all is well" system 40

benign allowing 104
best friend, you as your own 75
blessing in disguise 148–9
Brach, Tara 89, 120
brain:
    "No" 32
    and repetition 96
    social-care circuit 57
    social-engagement system 32
breathing exercises 45, 144
Buddhist tradition 10, 33, 78, 83, 124, 152, 164

Calhoun, Lawrence G 192
case studies:
    alcoholism 188–90
    anger 101–3
    anxiety 168–71
    bereavement 12–15, 86–7, 112–15, 158–62,
      166–7, 193
    cancer 144–5
    childbirth, fear of 186–7
    depression 93–5, 166–7
    divorce 68, 69–71, 69–74, 118–19
    facing up to own death 204–5
    infertility 140–2
    infidelity 38–42
    laid-off work 196–7
    panic attacks 50, 60–3
    resentment 112–15
    smoking 174–5
    suicide 193
    weight loss 93–5
Chan Khong 83
common humanity 53, 126
compassion 65, 70, 72, 79, 82, 122–3, 214
The Compassionate Friends 14
Confucius 48
A Course in Miracles (Williamson) 127
Covey, Stephen 202–3

Davidson, Richard 68
Death to Life 126

Dharamsala conference (1990) 88
dietary metamorphosis 110–11
Dyer, Wayne 6

enthusiastic embrace 176
extreme self-love 104

fight-or-flight 32
First Noble Truth 10
forgiveness 27, 126, 127

Gaelic tradition 215
Gandhi, Mahatma 144
"The Guest House" 67

Hebb, Donald 53
At Hell's Gate (Thomas) 83
higher power 104
Hindu tradition 172–3
Hume, David 132
hurt, hurt bred by 120

I Feel Pretty 90, 91
I Love you, You're Perfect, Now Change 111
Immanuel, Leia 91
impermanence 150–1
Internal Family Systems 100

Johnson, Mary 126
Jung, Carl 34, 210

karma 176–7
Katie, Byron 138
King, Martin Luther, Jr 194
Kübler-Ross, Elizabeth 28

letting go 44
Look for the Window (Bush) 192
loving-kindness practice 124–5
Loving What Is (Katie) 138

McGonigal, Kelly 198
metta bhavana 124–5
minimal resistance 138
Moonstruck 70

"name it to tame it" 55
Neff, Kristin 53, 60
neuroplasticity 96
"Next?" phase 41
Nietzsche, Friedrich Wilhelm 182
"No", letting go of 41, 43
Noble Truth 10

On Death and Dying (Kübler-Ross) 28

panic attacks 50–1, 60–2, 63
Plato 108
Plum Village 82
possibility paradox 41
post-traumatic stress disorder (PTSD) 82
"The Power of Mindfulness" (TED) 96
The Power of Now (Tolle) 134
power tools:
    ACT practice 76
    bittersweet memories 180
    connection stretch 179
    future-self exercise 208
    the glad game 206–7
    glass half full 128–9
    go with the flow 154
    heartfelt mantra exercise 107
    Ho'oponopono 130
    imagining "receiving compassion" exercise 78
    imagining "sending compassion" exercise 79
    journal reflection 131
    mirror exercise 107
    Pause. Breathe. Smile 155
    a reflection 46
    relaxing breathing sequence 46
    sensory grounding 178
    time travel exercise 106
    a visualization 44, 209
    writing exercise 155
Prentiss, Chris 152
Proust, Marcel 22

Radical Acceptance (Brach) 89, 120
"real" self 90
reincarnation 176–7
resilience 8, 32, 53
resistance 28, 29, 30, 32–4, 63, 67, 134, 138, 184

Rogers, Carl 80
rope, how to release 10–11, 33
Rumi 11

Salzberg, Sharon 88
Schwartz, Richard C 100
seasonal affective disorder (SAD) 143
second person, benefits of using for self 59
self-fulfilling prophecy 153
Set It Up 116
The 7 Habits of Highly Effective People (Covey)
    202–3
Shakespeare, William 197
shift questions 199
Siegel, Dan 32, 55
spiralling 196–7
suffering, defined 33

Taylor, Shelley E 57
TED talks 96, 198
Tedeschi, Richard G 192
"tend and befriend" 57
The Tending Instinct (Taylor) 57
Thich Nhat Hahn 82
Thomas, Claude Anshin 82–4, 98, 164
Thoreau, Henry David 156
Tolle, Eckhart 134
Transcending Loss (Bush) 192
12-step programmes 28, 166

unavoidable circumstances 136, 137
unlikely teachers 121
"The Upside of Stress" (TED) 198

"what is" 32, 36, 44, 211
What the Bleep Do We Know!? 198
Whitman, Walt 91
Williamson, Marianne 127
Winfrey, Oprah 134

"Yes" experience 32, 41, 43, 212
The Yes Man 212

Zen 83, 85, 152, 164
Zen and the Art of Happiness (Prentiss) 152

ACKNOWLEDGEMENTS

It takes a village to publish a book, and I'm blessed beyond measure to be working with the talented team at Octopus Publishing, who are outstanding in every regard.

I first want to acknowledge, with gratitude, my amazing editor, Leanne Bryan who, once again, believed in my message. What a joy to work with her, linking our visions together to make a dream a reality! And a huge thank you to Polly Poulter for her project management expertise, and to Juliette Norsworthy, the art director who helped to make this book absolutely gorgeous. Additionally, I extend my deep gratitude to Alison Wormleighton, Corinne Masciocchi, MFE Editorial Services, Miranda Harvey, Giulia Hetherington, Jennifer Veall and Allison Gonsalves for their talented contributions.

I also want to acknowledge, with great delight, John Willig, my literary agent extraordinaire. He is everything you could ever desire in a literary agent—and more. I am grateful for his hearty enthusiasm and ongoing support, and I appreciate his open, tenacious spirit.

I give thanks for my mother and father, my five children, my siblings and all the dear friends and family who have encouraged, supported and loved me along the way.

I bow, Namaste-style, to my soul sister Martha, an instrument of sacred light and love in all ways. I am so blessed to share the journey with her.

It is my joy to give thanks to the brothers of the Society of St John the Evangelist (SSJE), an Anglican monastic order, who have provided safe harbour and spiritual inspiration to me for nearly two decades.

I give thanks to the many other wise and inspired clinicians and researchers whose work has informed my own and who have led the way in understanding the importance of self-compassion, mindfulness, acceptance and inner peace.

I give thanks for my clients through these many years—you have taught me so much about life (and death) and have offered me the privilege of being your companion on deep and profound journeys of the heart and soul.

And finally, absolutely saving the best for last, I give thanks for my soul mate, best friend, colleague, first editor, lover and husband, Daniel Bush. You have filled my life with abundant love and effervescent magic. Every book that I write enters the world under your direct care, support and editorial guidance. I am richly blessed to have you as my partner in all aspects of life, both here and beyond.

PICTURE CREDITS